SO-ASK-545

PARABLES
FOR A NEW MILLENNIUM

PRESENTED BY
LONNIE MELASHENKO

WRITTEN BY
DAVID B. SMITH

Published by:
Voice of Prophecy
101 W. Chochran Street
Simi Valley, CA 93065

Cover design by Zero Crossing Graphics

Cover photo of gang member: Kurt Reichenbach

ISBN 0-9703940-0-4

Printed in the United States of America

Contents

Diary of a Prodigal Father

1
IT'S DAD'S MONEY WE'RE ALL SPENDING

He is so mad he can hardly see straight. I mean, this guy is red-in-the-face furious at the whole world. I'm talking, of course, about a little guy named Calvin, superhero of the late, great cartoon strip, *Calvin and Hobbes*. Creator Bill Watterston, for a number of years, delightfully captured the thought processes of this wild little boy who had such a vivid imagination that he conjured up a reality tiger, Hobbes, out of a stuffed toy.

But in this particular strip, Calvin is just fuming mad. When bed-time comes — always too soon, of course — he asks his dad: "Why can't I stay up late? You guys can!"

And there's no answer. "It's not fair!" he cries out to the world in general, his screaming mouth filling up the entire cartoon frame. Dad casually clears his throat. "The world isn't fair, Calvin." As if that fixed anything.

And the scowling rebel stalks off, his shoulders sagging. "I know," he admits, still spitting nails in his frustration. "But why isn't it ever unfair in my favor?"

And if there's any place in the Word of God almost guaranteed to make a person mad, it's the parables of Jesus. They reek of unfair-ness! They're absolutely loaded with undeserved favors: people finding treasures they didn't earn, bad boys getting to come back home, guys working one hour and getting paid for the whole day. "The first shall be last and the last shall be first." If you're the kind of person who has a built-in sense of fairness and justice and "a day's pay for a day's work," the parables of Jesus Christ are an absolutely stupid collection of stupid stories designed to make you see red. And that's all there is to it. They're awful!

Author Morris Venden was so struck by this fact that he wrote an

entire book a few years ago entitled *Parables of the Kingdom*.
And he comments very openly about the upside-down mentality of
God's kingdom. "The kingdom of heaven is on the gift system —
the kingdoms of earth are based on merit and on earning your own
rewards. The kingdom of heaven offers service for others as the
highest privilege — the earthly kingdoms seek service from others
as evidence of highest honor. The heavenly kingdom works
through the freedom of love — the kingdoms of earth use force to
accomplish their goals."

And really, that first line says it all. "The kingdom of heaven is on
the gift system." Over and over again, these maddening little stories tell us that many, many wide-eyed people are going to get
something good — something they don't deserve. When all the
redeemed walk through the pearly gates into heaven, there will be
quite a number of "thieves on crosses" . . . people who get into
heaven at the very last second, who didn't do a single thing to
merit even a hanky, let alone a glorious robe of victory. They
don't deserve a torn and tattered tent, let alone a mansion beyond
all imaginings. And yet here we are, standing on a sea of glass,
when we should be down in a much warmer and more unpleasant
climate.

Of course, these strange, Twilight Zone stories are only aggravat-
ing and irritating until you're the person who *receives* these undeserved treats. Our little friend Calvin howled out in his anger:
"Why isn't it ever unfair in MY favor?" And in all these stories
told by Jesus, the unfairness comes pouring into our own front
doors, in our favor every time.

But the story that has to be the epitome of it all is this one: *Diary
of a Prodigal Father*. Oh, I know that in the Bible, it's the "prodigal son." But it's very clear that in the end, it was the Dad who
was the most prodigal, not the son. Get out your dictionary and
we'll see.

This famous, often-told story is one you can find in Luke 15. There's a dad and there are two sons — the older son, and the famous one who ran off. He's the prodigal son. *And here's how* Jesus tells the story to His spellbound audience: "The younger [son] said to his father, 'Father, give me my share of the estate.' So he divided his property between them."

Now, right away this is very strange. When does a son generally inherit the family ranch? Not until Dad has passed away, of course. So this son, underneath the narrative line, is saying a couple things here. First of all: "I can't wait!" And really he's saying to Dad: "I wish you were dead. I don't like being your son; I don't like living here; I want out."

Here's the irony — and of course, this lands on your doorstep and mine. How often do God's people — the sons and daughters of God — decide they don't want that relationship any longer? "I'm leaving," we say to ourselves. "God, You leave me alone, and I'll leave You alone too. Because I want out of here." And yet with the very same breath, we tell God that we want an inheritance from Him. We want the family fortune: money, good health, prosperity, a college education, a new car, a wardrobe, and all the rest — FROM GOD. We say to Him: "Give me this and this and this and this . . . and then I'm going to leave." And wonder of wonders, just like in this story, a loving Dad goes along with such an incredibly selfish demand. He gives wicked people, rebellious earthlings who want to travel out of His jurisdiction, the family fortune! Have you seen fabulously wealthy people on television, on the evening news, who were very clearly living life separate from their heavenly Father? And yet they were wearing on their bodies the beautiful clothes God blessed them with resources to buy. Every breath they were taking was a gift from God; the beating of their hearts was God's present to them, an inheritance. And without so much as a "thanks a lot," they headed to Beverly Hills and the land of many parties.

And so does this bad boy of Luke 15. This dumb dad gives his boy what he wants: his half of the family fortune. And just a few days later, Son #2 does what he intended: he packs up and leaves. In fact, the Bible describes his departure this way: "Not long after that, the younger son got together all he had, set off for a distant country and there squandered his wealth in wild living."

There's an understated permanence to this whole expedition, isn't there? First of all, the math of the real world says this: once you get the inheritance from Pop, that's it, man. You've got it. There's not more where it came from. You get your share and you leave, and there's no coming back, because you got your share. That's the math of our world. And this boy leaves home with that understanding. He's not just going on a three-day, two-night junket to Vegas for a quick bit of fun. He's leaving forever. The Bible says: "He got together *all he had*."

And right here I notice something very wonderful. A person of this world might very well head off to a far country, determined that they're through with God. I mean, they are through! And they say so! "Father, I'm leaving and I'm not going to be back." Their plane ticket is one-way, and so is their mind-set and the jut of their jaw.

Pastor George Vandeman, who hosted the *It Is Written* television program for a number of years, tells how in his youth he actually shook his fist at heaven. "Leave me alone!" he screamed at God. "Holy Spirit, go away! And don't come back!" Here was another young rebel who got on the bus for what he was absolutely sure was a one-way ride to the devil's Disneyland. But you know, sometimes our God holds that return ticket stub in His hand and just doesn't say anything for quite a long while.

In any case, the young man gets to the faraway country and proceeds to spend his dad's fortune in loose living. He quickly blows the entire bundle on booze and babes and blackjack and bubbly burgundy wine. And let me emphasize the same sober truth again: this is his father's money he's spending. Dad gave him some wonderful gifts, and he spent them in Las Vegas.

You know, every time we waste a talent, or drop a dollar where we shouldn't, do we remember that this was a gift from a loving Father? Right now you might be a rebel on your own journey. But every ability you've got — your earning power, your personality, your skills and talents, your friendships — those are all gifts God gave you. At the moment you may be spending them very badly; the inheritance you were given might be going right into the dealer's tray at the roulette wheel. God gave you gifts and you wasted them. Shame on you and shame on all of us.

And yet the story doesn't end right here. In our terms, in our math, it would. You lose your money, you pawn your car, you go broke, and that's it. But in these parables of Jesus, everything is upside-down. Where a story would usually end, this one is just getting started. Where normal math would say, "You're busted, mister," this story goes in a whole different direction. No wonder a recent bestseller by Philip Yancey, entitled *What's So Amazing About Grace?*, has this for a chapter title: "The New Math of Grace."

Coming right up, we'll sample God's way of adding up the numbers.

2
WHERE HAVE ALL THE FRIENDS GONE?

There was a very disquieting article in the March 16, 1998 edition of *Newsweek* entitled "Heaven's Gatekeepers." Several New Age authors had really hit the big-time, and their books on the topic of communicating with spirits were riding high on the New York Times bestseller charts.

In one in particular, entitled "Talking to Heaven," people are pretty much guaranteed eternal life, no matter who or what they might have believed in here on earth. The spirits of our departed friends and relatives are all around us; a grieving mother who comes to this man for comfort has him contact the spirit of her dead little girl. "I see figures on the wallpaper," he says. "Yes. She's talking about . . . rabbits. The bunny rabbits." And the mother almost weeps for joy: yes, there were rabbits on the wallpaper in her little girl's room.

In this same article, a very thought-provoking assertion is made: "[This author] holds out the promise of eternal life after death without the necessity of believing in Jesus or in anything else beyond the grasp of an average dog or cat."

And he goes on to assert that everyone — I mean, everyone — including Adolf Hitler, will be in heaven. He mentions Hitler by name as being a person who will be saved in heaven.

Well, this is quite a distance removed from our parable of the prodigal son. And yet we find that this New Age claim of eternal life isn't that far afield. Because in Jesus' story, here was a young man who repudiated his father. "Dad, I want your money," he said. "But I don't want you. I don't want to be your son; I don't want any relationship with you. Nothing but half of your estate. And then I'm out of here."

Then this kid took off — in his mind, permanently — chartered a limousine to a faraway land, and then proceeded to live a life of profligate spending with his father's money. He wouldn't take Dad, but he would take Dad's money. And he was certainly very happy to spend Dad's money.

Of course, right here in the story is where many of us find ourselves. You know, everything we have came to us from God. Our money, our abilities, our health, our friends, our homes, all of our comforts, every meal we eat. The Bible talks over and over about how all good gifts come from God. "Every good and perfect gift is from above," it says in James 1:17.

And yet we find in the human race a strong proclivity to spend those gifts, not just apart from God, but in active defiance of Him and in opposition to His kingdom. We almost use His money to fund the rebel, anti-heaven campaign. As these New Age superstars suggest, a person can live life without God, either making millions on the talk-show circuit, or maybe even feeding the fires of the Auschwitz ovens . . . and still get an inheritance of eternal life from God.

So let's say this prodigal son traveled to Las Vegas' Glitter Gulch to spend his dad's fortune. Which reminds me of an old comedy record album from Bill Cosby, who once addressed a ballroom of vacationers and gamblers in one of the Nevada hotels. And he pointed out how many of them would spend their whole weekend out in the casino playing cards at the 21 tables, praying to God. "Oh, God, give me an eight. Give me a five. Give me a ten down for this double-down." And then he scolded, tongue-in-cheek: "And ain't none of you going to then go to church Sunday morning. Not if you're winning." In other words, they had this prodigal-son attitude: Take God's money and His blessings . . . and then do your own thing.

Keep a thumb in Luke 15 and this colorful parable, but just a few pages earlier is another of God's principles enumerated for us to consider. Listen, have you received gifts and talents from God? Of course you have. We all have. We owe God everything, and the more gifted you might be, the more you owe. Luke 12:48: "From everyone who has been given much, much will be demanded; and from the one who has been entrusted with much, much more will be asked." That's actually the tag line to more than one of Jesus' parables, but considered in this story right here, it reminds us of the fact that we are all in this adventure together. We're all that runaway son. We're all spending, one way or another, a fortune a loving Parent gave to us.

Even before we hit the PLAY button on our VCRs and continue with the story, let me just encourage you and me both. Let's live in relationship with the Father who gave us these gifts. So often people pray, to this distant Father, and they really do want an answer. But they don't want anything more than the answer. They don't want the God who provides the answer. They might pray for healing; they might beg heaven for a mate or for a job. It might even be a pretty good prayer, an unselfish prayer — healing for a child or a friend. They might pray for forgiveness of sins, for guilty feelings to be gone. Even Judas Iscariot once cried out in desperation: "I have sinned!" But it's still a prayer with the most important part clipped off: they don't want a relationship. They don't want anything more than the return package in the mail. They want a kind of free New Age eternity without a life lived in devotion to Jesus Christ, without a surrendered heart.

But now back to this kid. Because very quickly the money runs out. The merry-go-round stops spinning. And isn't that true of all Satan's promises? "I'll give you knowledge," he said to Eve. And true, she did learn about a few new things: thorns, pain, sorrow, her first son killing her second one. And then she died herself.

"I'll give you fun," he says to people today. And there is fun out there in Lucifer's playground. Champagne glasses clink together and pretty girls offer their services to someone who's spending God's fortune in Satan's kingdom. But when the fortune runs out, so does the fun. King Solomon once lamented: "I tried everything. I had everything. And it was all vanity. Meaningless. Unfulfilling." A man had 700 wives and 300 girlfriends, and couldn't find fulfillment. And that's the eventual discovery of every prodigal son or daughter.

Well, in verse 14 two things hit the prodigal son all at once. Not only does his money run out, but a famine hits. And our young hero hadn't planned for either of these events. But right here we discover yet another contrast between the math of the world and the math of God's kingdom. Because here on earth, on Tropicana Boulevard in Las Vegas, people are connected to each other by what? By a man's bankroll. For nights on end, this boy's existence was flavored by one expression: "Drinks are on me." He had friends because the drinks were on him. People were connected to him because of money. Which is fine; that's how the world operates. We go to work for a company because they agree to pay us. We hang around with certain people because they have things we like or because their presence makes us feel important. We're kind to our aging relatives because we know they have wills and sports cars and mountain cottages to give away. These are the strands that connect us to one another; this is the mathematics of a sinful race.

And this young man found out with a vengeance that in Sin City, A always leads to B. Money leads to Friends; No Money leads to No Friends. And when he got down to his last quarter, all of his so-called friends crossed the street to another casino. That's the fundamental math equation in Satan's textbook.

So the prodigal son finds himself having to work for a living. Which, once you've departed from the kingdom of God, is the way of the world too. That's Economics 101 here on planet earth: when there's a famine on and you've run out of Daddy's money, you get a job, Buster. Any job you can get. Salvation by works. And this young man, now reduced to wearing rags, bums a Classified section out of a trash can and finds that the only job listings have to do with feeding pigs. That's right! This kid, born and raised as an orthodox Jew, now has to feed the most unclean animal of all. He's a pig-keeper, and soon he's so hungry he's tempted to eat the pigs' food, the pods from the carob trees. Things are that bad.

In the King James Version, verse 15 says: "And he went and joined himself to a citizen of that country; and he sent him into his fields to feed swine."

The Greek word, kollaō, which gives us "joined himself to" actually can mean "to glue together" or "join" or "to cleave to." In essence, this starving young man now has to basically sell himself off as a slave to the owner of the pig farm, this citizen of a faraway country. He's a slave now! Where once he lived in freedom with Dad, having access to all of Dad's love and wealth and wisdom, now he's a slave to someone in the enemy camp. More of Satan's math — where a person trades in freedom for slavery, the holdings of heaven for the leftover scraps of a pig's dinner.

So far the equation is holding up about as expected. But the whole story's about to turn upside-down.

3
HEAVEN'S WAKE-UP CALLS

The National Geographic book, *Everest: Mountain Without Mercy*, describes how a pathologist named Beck Weathers was lost on the world's highest mountain in the killing season of May 1996. A number of climbers were already dead, and he was lying comatose in the snow just 350 yards away from Camp Four. Another climber, Yasuko Namba, lay nearby; the rest of his party had struggled through the horrific blizzard winds back to their tents.

It was the evening of May 10 when he and the others got lost there on the South Col. The next morning, with the winds abating just a bit, a couple of climbers managed to stagger out to where the two lost climbers were lying in the snow. To their surprise, the two were still breathing, but just barely. Neither one had much of a pulse; their eyes were glazed over, their limbs frozen. With heavy hearts, the climbers decided that it just wasn't possible to even try to rescue them. The scant resources of oxygen and human strength they had left had better be reserved for stronger climbers. "It was a classic case of triage," one wrote later.

It wasn't long before Namba finally breathed her last. And yet for hours this Texan, Beck Weathers, lay there in the snow, completely comatose. And then all at once, for some reason no one can explain, something flickered in his brain. He "came to."

Somehow a light went on and he regained consciousness. He stared at this odd blue object, which he suddenly realized was his own completely frozen hand. And he slowly grew aware of where he was: near the top of Everest with no one around. He finally recognized that, as he put it later, the cavalry wasn't about to come get him and if he was going to be saved, he would have to get up and walk back through his almost snow-blinded condition into camp. Which is precisely what he did. In a feat of courage they're still talking about, this stubborn doctor figured out by wind currents which way it was to the tents. And like a mummy in a horror movie, he slowly shuffled through the blizzard and into the camps of safety. He later lost both hands, one forearm, and a nose — but is alive.

And it's that moment of "coming to" which interests us here. Beck Weathers can't explain it. Normally he should have just slowly lapsed into unconsciousness and then a peaceful death. But right when he needed a jolt of some kind, it was provided there at 26,000 feet. Something or Someone said to him: "Wake up."
In the story of the prodigal son, our young man has gotten to the identical point. Lost on the mountain. In his case, he was lost on the pig farm. And it isn't just a case of being out in the middle of nowhere; this boy has simply gone into a moral stupor. For months, maybe years, he's been so blind he couldn't see what was what. He left what was good, and ran off to sample that which was bad. He left safety for danger; security for risk, God for Satan. True love for false, real friends for phony ones. A full table for starvation.

And now here are six wonderful words found in Luke 15:17: "When he came to his senses . . ." In the King James Version, it says: "And when he came to himself . . ."

And all through God's Word, we find this shuddering moment replayed over and over. King Solomon had it hit him after years of being in a moral stupor of concubines and idolatry. His father, King David, was jolted right off his throne when a prophet named Nathan pointed a finger in his face and shouted: "Thou art the man!" Saul, later to be the apostle Paul, was breezing along the road to Damascus, his conscience stuck in neutral, when a bright light from heaven knocked him off his horse of spiritual complacency.

In this Bible parable of the prodigal son, Luke 15 doesn't say anything about the father's intervention at this point. Dad is simply waiting back home, going out to the mailbox each day and looking down the road for his son. But I'd like to suggest that in the real story — which is you and me — that moment of "coming to our senses" is one that is caused by the Father every time. We don't wake ourselves up. Just as God sent the prophet Nathan with that forceful wake-up call to an adulterous king, He jolts this prodigal son. "That's enough," He says. "Wake up!"

Through what means does a heavenly Father do this? Well, He does have His prophets: men and women whose warnings are direct communiques from heaven. How many of us have been reading in our Bibles, when all at once a verse leaped out at us and gave a strong spiritual pinch. And after we said, "Ouch!", we fell on our knees and thanked God for putting that verse there specifically for us. Has that happened to you? It certainly has happened to me . . . many times. And I didn't enjoy it, but I thank God that He has caused me to "come to my senses." Even when I'm composing radio scripts, there have been times when the messages which were written and intended for you turned around and became God's loving missile for me instead.

God also uses His own Holy Spirit as an active agent to wake up comatose climbers on the Mount Everest of the spiritual journey. And I believe He even uses heaven-sent trials and hard times, if necessary, to jar a man or even an entire nation to repentance.

Recently at our Thursday Morning Worldwide Prayer Circle, someone brought in a letter with a most unusual sentiment expressed in it. It was from a man named Terry, and from the look of the envelope and the unusual address, we could tell that this was from a prisoner. Sure enough, inside there was a three-page letter from an inmate here in our California Department of Corrections. But here's the sentence that made everyone sit up straight.

"Dear Voice of Prophecy: Prison has been a great and wonderful experience for me."

And maybe we say, "What! He likes it in there? Is this guy on the psych ward?" No, because here's how he finishes that sentence. "Prison has been a great and wonderful experience for me . . . and I thank God for His loving chastisement."

Most of his three-page letter is filled with praise to Christ and Bible verses. But you see, there's just a tiny and humble glimpse into his former life. And it almost sounds word-for-word like the story of the prodigal son. He writes about ". . . the self-destructive life that I lived once I hit the big city with its mountain-high buildings, late nights, wild parties, and dark alleys. And oh! we must not forget the stones . . . crack [cocaine.] How could I sink so low? By resisting the call of God over and over again. I ran right into the open arms of the devil."

But now this man is a vibrant, witnessing, born-again Christian, praising God that he is in prison! Praising God that somehow there went off a heavenly wired light bulb in his brain. And like that prodigal son, he had a "V-8 moment" where he smacked himself in the head and said: "Where have I been? What could I have been thinking? Why was I so foolish? All at once I realize what I could have had!"

Most people have to get clear down to bottom before this "coming to the senses" happens. If we think there's any way, any way at all, to survive on our own, we're going to do it. We have to be feeding the pigs, so to speak, or down to our last empty oxygen canister on Everest, before we realize that we've run out of options. The son in this story doesn't finally think about going home until he's completely given up on himself. He has no money left. No food. No earning power. No friends. He's in a pit and absolutely cannot get a toehold.

And finally he says to himself in verse 17: "How many of my father's hired men have food to spare, and here I am starving to death! I will set out" — in the King James it says, "I will arise"

— "and go back to my father and say to him: 'Father, I have sinned against heaven and against you. I am no longer worthy to be called your son; make me like one of your hired men.'"

And you know, here is just the clearest picture of the human response. This is giving up without really giving up! Notice: he has a little speech planned, and some things in it are right. "I have sinned." That's for sure true. "I'm not worthy to be your son." That's even more true; after all, he's used up the inheritance that would be his by rights. He's depleted the family tank of "sonship." So he knows he's in bad shape. According to the math of this world, he's down to zero and below. He's well down in the negative numbers.

And yet what's his plan? "I'll go home and work! I'll qualify to be a servant! I'll at least earn some food and maybe a warm bed. I know I can't be a son anymore; that option's lost to me. But I still have a strong body; I can get a job at Dad's place and earn a day's pay for a day's work."

So this broken-down guy surrenders about the way most of us do. "I'm helpless," we admit. "But maybe I'm not *completely* helpless. I still have some earning power with God. I can come back to Him and do some odd jobs around the house, maybe at least get into the servants' quarters, and then take it from there."

So he starts out. But you know, this young man's about to receive the New Math explosion of his life.

4
A PARTY IN TRAVERSE CITY, MICHIGAN

In his gripping bestseller entitled *What's So Amazing About Grace?*, Philip Yancey has a passage where he rewrites the story of the prodigal son. And on the back jacket of the book, a reviewer named Brennan Manning has this to say:

"[This is] the crown jewel of all [Yancey's] books." And then comes this warning: "If you read the chapter, 'The Lovesick Father,' and do not weep for joy, I suggest you check your pulse . . . or make an appointment with your mortician."

And then Yancey tells his story, of how a young girl in Traverse City, Michigan, decides that Dad is stupid and home is stupid and church is stupid, and she wants to leave for the big city. So she does. She runs away, goes to Detroit, and ends up making a living the same way many other homeless girls do. A guy with a big car — "The Boss" — gets her all set up with a nice penthouse suite, with room service and limo rides and men who pay handsomely for the tricks she knows.

But drugs wear down her body, and soon, with the dark circles under her eyes, she can't command the same prices as before. The next day The Boss throws her out, and things get harder and harder. Soon she's sleeping on metal grates outside department stores through a hard Detroit winter.

And finally she has the moment of coming to her senses. "Maybe I'll go home," she says to herself. So she calls, but just gets the answering machine. "Dad, Mom, it's me," she says. "I was wondering about maybe coming home. I'm catching a bus up your way, and it'll get there about midnight tomorrow. If you're not there, well, I guess I'll just stay on the bus until it hits Canada." So she rides. And she rides. And she practices over and over the speech, how she's sorry. She'd been so foolish. Can you ever forgive me? And as the bus gets closer, her heart is pounding. What if they never even got the message? What if they're not there? They get to Traverse City, and she realizes that the next fifteen minutes will decide her life. And it's pure terror for her.

According to the math of the world, she ought to get nothing. Zip. And she knows it. No forgiveness, no welcome back, no making up for how she's slapped everyone in the face. Is that how it will be? Or will Dad be there?

Here's the finish to the story, in Yancey's own words: "She walks into the terminal not knowing what to expect. Not one of the thousand scenes that have played out in her mind prepare her for what she sees. There, in the concrete-walls-and-plastic-chairs bus terminal in Traverse City, Michigan, stands a group of forty brothers and sisters and great-aunts and uncles and cousins and a grandmother and great-grandmother to boot. They're all wearing goofy party hats and blowing noise-makers, and taped across the entire wall of the terminal is a computer-generated banner that reads 'Welcome home!'

"Out of the crowd of well-wishers breaks her Dad. She stares out through the tears quivering in her eyes like hot mercury and begins the memorized speech, 'Dad, I'm sorry. I know . . .' He interrupts her. 'Hush, child. We've got no time for that. No time for apologies. You'll be late for the party. A banquet's waiting for you at home.'"

End of story. In the Bible, and on page 51 of this wonderful, wonderful book entitled *What's So Amazing About Grace?* But right here you and I can simply get out the biggest trash bin we can find and throw into it every math textbook we can find. Every book about philosophy. Every book about sensible business principles.

Every calculator which says that two and two is four. Every diary where a record is kept of someone else's wrongs. Every scorecard, every set of scales where things ought to balance. And you just keep throwing out and throwing out because this strange and wonderful story of the prodigal son just turns the universe upside-down.

Because here's a kid who deserves nothing. Nothing! He already got his share! And he used it up! He burned his account down to zero! And he staggers home, knowing full well that he deserves zero in return. His only hope is to maybe get minimum wage, $5.75 an hour, working on Dad's farm. He doesn't even deserve that after all the "I hate you's" he shouted on his way out.

But here in verse 20 we discover the New Math of heaven: "But while he was still a long way off, his father saw him and was filled with compassion for him; he ran to his son, threw his arms around him and kissed him."

And now comes the stupid speech. "The son said to him, 'Father, I have sinned against heaven and against you. I am no longer worthy to be called your son." But the father said to the son, "Shut up. Just shut up." (Actually, I added that part. Here's verse 22, though.) "But the father said to his servants, 'Quick! Bring the best robe and put it on him. Put a ring on his finger and sandals on his feet. Bring the fattened calf and kill it. Let's have a feast and celebrate. For this son of mine was dead and is alive again; he was lost and is found."

I guess math-wise, this is a stupid story. Psychology-wise, this is a stupid story. I imagine even the late Dr. Benjamin Spock would say, "That is a stupid story." But here is the mathematics of heaven! A kid uses up the whole family fortune, but Dad takes him back and restores him to a whole new fortune. Not as a servant; not a prison parolee with a record to live down. He's back as a son!

In his book, *Parables of the Kingdom*, Morris Venden points out how all three of the dad's gifts right here are hugely symbolic. The boy says, "I have sinned." And he receives a rich robe to cover the shame of his sins, his rags. He says, "I'm not worthy to be your son." But the dad doesn't even hear him; he immediately gives the boy his signet ring to wear, a symbol of reinstatement in the family. The boy, hardly able to get in a word edgewise, says, "Dad, wait. Let me just be a servant." But before he can finish the sentence, Dad has him in a brand new pair of shoes . . . and of course, in that Judean culture, the servants and slaves didn't wear shoes; they went barefoot. Only a trusted son would have shoes on. This father gives his son the very gifts that demonstrate the wonderfully strange, different mathematics of heaven, God's equation of grace.

Maybe you've been wondering since we started about this title: *Diary of a Prodigal Father.* Isn't it the son who was prodigal? Is this a typo? I want to dip back into an old VOP radio script where we told a story that came out in the video stores in 1997. A young man who's basically spurned his wife finally comes to his senses. "How could I have been so foolish?" he wonders. "She loved me so much and I didn't realize! I will arise . . . and go home to her." And at the house he tries to find her in the crowd. "Hello — I'm looking for my wife." And he begins this long prodigal-son speech: "I was so foolish. I need you. Please forgive me. Please take me back." And he goes on for about three minutes, until she cuts him off. "Just shut up," she says very softly. And then, just like the dad in this story, she adds: "You had me at 'hello.'" She throws out the old math of revenge and divorce and I-want-so-much-alimony, and says to the man she loves with such an incredible love: "Jerry Maguire, shut up with your foolish, unnecessary speech. Because you had me at 'hello.'"

And so who is it who is prodigal? Did you know what *prodigal* really means? It refers to wild, reckless, wasteful, lavish spending. Giving profusely. Abundantly overflowing generosity. Which the son in this story certainly did during his Las Vegas days. But how much more "prodigal" is the Dad . . . in how much he loves! After giving away the family fortune, which is frittered away, the son who returns is handed the keys to the bank again! Talk about prodigal! Talk about excessive! This is truly the story of the prodigal Dad.

And every one of us is in this story. We've all taken the inheritance down to zero. Not one of us has anything good in us to recommend us to the Dad we rejected. Oh, you may still have a few dollars left of good deeds and obedience and so-called loyalty left in your pocket. But the Bible teaches that we're all sinners.

We've all wandered away. And we've all dreamed of making a comeback in our own power, or at least getting hired on as servants next time instead of sons and daughters.

And maybe this story right here is God's way of waking you up. You can't even get home by yourself, but Dad has a return ticket for you. And it absolutely does not matter what you've done. A hundred sins, a million, a *billion*. Small or big. White lies or huge lies. Small sins or vile offenses. Doesn't matter. Pile them up as high as you can; doesn't matter. Make a list as long as the Constitution; doesn't matter. Because the math of heaven, the grace of God, the prodigal love of the Father simply throws it all out. You start with your speech, and God tells you to stop. He's not interested in that. He just wants to get started with the robe and the ring and the shoes and the party.

That's one more thing about the math of heaven: they seem to be able to afford an awful lot of parties.

5
A WRONG TURN TO INDIA

As we finish up with the prodigal son, I have to get up my courage to tell you about a very foolish man. I mean, this guy is really kind of dumb. I know that sounds crude, but wait until you hear about him.

His name is Dr. Paul Brand — and I've mentioned him on radio broadcasts before, usually in a more generous vein. But here I'm telling you, he faced a crossroads in life, and took a nasty and ill-advised detour down the wrong road.

He got his degree in medicine in the year 1946, right after the war ended. And he was talented; no doubt about that. He's written some good bestsellers and had a noteworthy career. But right there at the start, he just plain and simple made a wrong choice. Instead of starting up a lucrative practice in London, he got suckered into traveling back to the land of his birth, and working in a hospital in Vellore, India.

Now, his family couldn't come with him for a whole six months. So he was out there in the middle of nowhere all by himself. Secondly, Vellore in 1946 wasn't exactly the Johns Hopkins Medical Center. He lived in a tiny little cubicle, taking baths by dipping a ladle into the water and then splashing it on himself. And then there was the heat. A hundred and ten degrees, all day, every day. Just breathing made a person sweat, he confessed later. Well, could he just switch on the air conditioning? Not in 1946 he couldn't. Nothing was air conditioned in Vellore, even in the oper-ating room. In fact, with the risk of infection, he and his fellow surgeons and nurses didn't even dare to have fans going. So they would stand there, dripping wet with perspiration, doing one oper-ation after another. Between each patient, they would go outside, step out of their sopping-wet gowns, change into dry ones, and then head right back into the sauna for another operation. And this was for 12-hour days.

In that kind of a climate, you really needed to drink at least six quarts a day, but Brand found that when he did so, he would break into a horrible "prickly heat" rash. Which, if you scratched at it, would turn into boils and infection. A fellow doctor advised him that if he cut back on the drinking, he would develop kidney stones instead. So that was the choice: kidney stones or painful rash. And most of the medical people had to go through bouts of dysentery, hepatitis, influenza, and a local disease called "dengue," more commonly referred to as "break-bone fever," because for about a week you felt like every bone in your body was broken. Well, that's the choice this foolish, misguided doctor made. Instead of practicing medicine in Beverly Hills, he was out there in Vellore, "working for Jesus." That was what his missionary spirit had led him to do.

As we think about the mathematics of God's kingdom and this story of the prodigal son, we haven't addressed yet the situation of the older brother. Because all of the math in this story works against him, doesn't it? His younger brother takes half the family inheritance, goes to a faraway place, and spends it like a drunken sailor. Then when he comes home, Dad simply rewrites the will so that he's back in it with a whole new inheritance. He scores twice! Meanwhile, this older brother, who had stayed on the farm, working away year after year, obeying the rules, toeing the mark, gets nothing. Oh, he got the regular inheritance . . . but he had that coming anyway. And as he points out to his father, he'd never been given so much as a goat so he could have a little barbecue party with his friends.

You know, several of these stories Jesus tells have a common theme where someone is a chump. In this story, it's the older brother. In another of Jesus' odd little tales, some guys work for the Master in the vineyard all day — speaking of 110 degrees — and then get the exact same pay as those who just worked in the shade for one hour right at quitting time.

So we surmise that these are the people who have served God the whole way. It's hot out there in the blazing sun of the mission field, and these men and women put in 60-hour weeks for maybe 50 years of service. And then they die, maybe of amoebic dysentery, and get a tiny little grave marker out in Bangladesh, while their counterparts are soaking in Hollywood Jacuzzis.

Peter, the disciple of Jesus, finally noticed that there were two kinds of people who were going to get into Jesus' kingdom. Suckers like himself, who put in a whole lifetime of work and obedience, and then people like this prodigal son. And contrary to some of the jokes you read in Christian magazines these days about who got to heaven and got a big mansion and who got there and had to sleep in a little chicken coop, Jesus Christ never talked about bigger houses for the faithful few. And so finally Peter asked him that very question. "Hey!" he protested. "We've left everything to follow You! What's in it for us?" In other words, if Calvary's gift of grace puts every single believer on the golden streets of the kingdom, then where's the extra reward for the older brother? For the missionary to India? For the person who works for God his whole life, instead of just slipping in under the wire like the thief on the cross?

I think we find some biblical understanding here by considering some of the characters we haven't addressed yet. And those are the servants of this estate owner. They live right there on the property, but they're not sons — instead, they're there for a wage. They put in 40 hours a week, punching a clock, wearing their uniforms, protected by the company's Delta Dental health plan, and once a week they get a check. Now, there's nothing wrong with this kind of a relationship, but it's not the same thing as being a son.

Remember that when the prodigal son first thought of coming

home, he had no inkling that he might get to be a son again. But he might get to stay out back in the servants' quarters, where there was heat in the winter, air conditioning in the summer, and three good meals a day, and that Blue Shield health plan. And he knew, deep down, that his father — former father, really — was a decent employer: fair, honest, reasonable. Working for Dad — actually, he would probably have to call him Mr. Jones now — wouldn't be that bad. Compared to feeding these pigs, anyway. And that's what he went back hoping to get: the relationship of an employee.

When you think about it, the older son was actually more like an employee than a son too. He obeyed, but he didn't enjoy it. He followed the rules, but didn't love the Rulegiver. He stayed on the farm because it was comfortable and because it was the status quo. And frankly, he stayed on the farm because he knew that he, too, had an inheritance coming. For him, those were the true "wages." If he put in his time until Dad died, and got the whole farm deeded to him, it'd be a lot more than minimum wage. So it was worth staying. Deep down, this guy was a glorified employee who just happened to have the same last name as the boss.

Morris Venden makes this observation: "The elder brother was a 'good liver.' But it isn't much fun being good in the way he was good. That kind of good living will put ulcers in your stomach and lines on your face, because badness held in check is not goodness, and never will be."

You know, some of us run the risk of being servants instead of sons too. Let me confess to you: I get a paycheck every two weeks from the church. I am paid from heaven's storehouses. I pay my rent and my grocery bill with money that, in a way, goes through heaven's financial savings-and-loan. And frankly, it would be rather easy — and surely a great tragedy — to begin to think of this radio job, this work at the Voice of Prophecy, as just that:

work. A medium-paying job for a 45-year-old man. A career where God is the boss and not the Father, an employer rather than a Friend.

The older brother in this parable betrays his feelings with a nasty little remark in verse 30. He's angry about Dad giving his younger brother a robe and a ring and a feast, and he says so. But notice his language:

"When this son of yours who has squandered your property with prostitutes comes home, you kill the fattened calf for him!" Notice: not "my brother." No, it's "this son of yours." This older brother doesn't even consider this to be a family anymore. Dad is an employer, not a father. And he certainly doesn't claim this renegade as his brother.

But the purpose of this parable is to lift up the joys of sonship! When you love your Dad, really love Him, then it's wonderful to be with Him in His vineyard. The longer the better! The more you get to serve with Him, the more rewarding! Wouldn't you rather have the whole day with this wonderful Father than just the last hour? Better, don't you think, to work a whole lifetime in joy for Jesus than just the last 15 minutes like the foolish thief on the cross? Really, who's the lucky one?

There's a surprising end to that story of Dr. Paul Brand, who made the "dumb" decision to go work in the steamy town of Vellore, India. This Christian wrote later: "Never had I felt so challenged and fulfilled. Some people look upon expatriate doctors in Third World countries as self-sacrificing heroes. I know better. Most are having the time of their lives."

For Dr. Paul Brand, the heat and the mosquitos and the sores and the endless surgeries were a mosaic of joy, because he was working for God and with God. Foolish? By the world's math, of course. Measured by heaven's yardstick, the man's a genius.

I Can't Afford Your Free Tuxedo

6
BLACK TIE ALL THE WAY

It happens fairly often when you stay in a downtown hotel. You're eating in the smallest coffee shop, trying to save a few dollars. Or maybe even hiking a couple of blocks to the nearest Wendy's. But there in the main ballroom of your hotel is a huge, gala, black-tie affair. They have punch-bowl fountains spraying out pink champagne; there's a dance band set up in one corner. The place is set with the finest china; bouquets are everywhere. And milling all around are 800 guests who are about to sit down to a $55-a-plate dinner.

Of course, you're not invited, but you do notice all of the glitter and the gold as you go back to your room with your Wendy's french fry wrappers and little packs of ketchup.

In Philip Yancey's book, *What's So Amazing About Grace?*, he shares an anecdote from the Boston Globe in June of 1990. A young lady had gone with her fiancé to the Hyatt Hotel there in town to order their wedding banquet. Both of them had Cadillac tastes, and before they'd finished picking this and that off the menu, they'd signed their names to a contract for a $13,000 shindig. So they wrote a check for half that amount as a down payment, and went home to start licking the wedding envelopes. Well, bad news. The very day the envelopes were supposed to go in the mail, the groom got cold feet. "I'm not sure," he said. "Let's wait; let's postpone."

The young woman, angry, of course, drove down to the Hyatt to try to call off the big black-tie party. But the events manager shook her head. "I'm sorry," she said. "But the way your contract is written, you're stuck. That's all there is to it. We could refund you ten percent — just thirteen hundred dollars — but the rest can't be returned."

Do you know what this Boston socialite decided to do? Since she was going to lose 90% of her thirteen grand anyway, she decided to go ahead and have the party. Not a wedding party anymore, thanks to her gutless boyfriend, but a party nonetheless. So she dug in her purse, paid the rest of the bill, and then hosted the biggest, boldest, most boogie-ing party Boston had ever seen . . . for all of the down-and-outers in the city.

That's right. Here's how Yancey caps off this odd, wonderful story: "And so it was that in June of 1990 the Hyatt Hotel in downtown Boston hosted a party such as it had never seen before. The hostess changed the menu to boneless chicken — 'in honor of the groom,' she said — and sent invitations to rescue missions and homeless shelters. That warm summer night, people who were used to peeling half-gnawed pizza off the cardboard dined instead on chicken cordon bleu. Hyatt waiters in tuxedos served *hors d'oeuvres* to senior citizens propped up by crutches and aluminum walkers. Bag ladies, vagrants, and addicts took one night off from the hard life on the sidewalks outside and instead sipped champagne, ate chocolate wedding cake, and danced to big-band melodies late into the night."

Well, it's a wonderful story, but really the first telling of this socially upside-down event comes from the mouth of Jesus Himself. *I Can't Afford Your Free Tuxedo.*

In Matthew 22, Jesus is right in the middle of telling several stories. And if you go back one chapter, you find that His main audience was not too friendly, made up mostly of priests and rabbis and the elders of the church. This was the religious establishment of the day, and we think of Pharisees and Sadducees and their hard, humorless faces, their eagerness to catch this Teacher from Galilee in a moment of heresy.

Well, Jesus begins to tell this Hyatt Hotel story. "The kingdom of heaven is like a king who prepared a wedding banquet for his son.

He sent his servants to those who had been invited to the banquet to tell them to come, but they refused to come."

We're always tempted, when we read stories like these, to immediately assign the characters. The king represents God, of course, and so the son in this wedding story would be Jesus Himself. No wonder Christ used parables! The priests and Pharisees would have never stood still for it if Jesus openly told this story on Himself.

Notice that we have here two invitations. Already an earlier invitation had been given, and now the king's servants went from door to door to the selected, upper-crust guests, just as a reminder, a follow-up invitation. One commentary noted that, even today, it's common in Oriental cultures to honor special guests by sending out personal envoys. And it's at least hinted that these envoys were knocking on the doors of people who had previously agreed to come. They'd already R.S.V.P.ed.

Who, then, would be the people on this first guest list? One might answer: "The children of Israel," since they were the original Chosen People. All through the Old Testament God had invited them to be in a special relationship with Himself. Through the Old Testament prophets and sacred writings, this first invitation had been sent. And certainly this first list of potential honorees would include the religious people of Christ's day: the priests, the teachers of truth. So it might well be that some of those standing there in the crowd hearing this story noted that they, too, were in the narrative.

"But they refused to come." Israel, of course, had said yes to God in a generic sense; maybe you remember that famous line right after God gave them the Ten Commandments at Mount Sinai: "All that the Lord has said, we will do." That's in Exodus 24. Here in Jesus' day, they certainly considered that they were full-fledged members of the wedding party. They were the seed of Abraham!

But when it came right down to honoring the Son of God, the Bridegroom, they said no. They couldn't make it after all.

So the generous king sent out some more limousines and hired a more prestigious messenger service. "Please do come," these ambassadors begged. "The king has gone to a lot of trouble. And this is for his son! You wouldn't want to miss that, would you? Please? You said you'd come. And plus, the king's already had the big dinner prepared; the steaks are sizzling and the Dom Perignon is chilled just right." (Non-alcoholic, of course.) Twice in a row here in these parables, we find a God who "kills the fatted calf." He spares no expense to show His feelings for the subjects in His kingdom.

And as Jesus tells the story, the people on God's A List just give a big shrug. "I can't make it," they say. *"Who Wants To Be a Millionaire?* is on that night, and I don't know how to program my VCR." "I've got to go check my field and see if my radishes are growing." "I've got to attend to my business affairs." Even though these people offer a pretense of loyalty to the king, and accept his protection and rulership, when it comes right down to it they don't want to honor him or his son. In fact, verse 6 says that some of these people grabbed the messengers, dragged them out of the palace limos, and beat them up. In a couple of neighborhoods, they even killed them! So this is nearly a state of civil war.

Interestingly, verse 7 does have one moment, one display, of royal strength. "The king was enraged. He sent his army and destroyed those murderers and burned their city."

There's a sober message right here. The King is loving and kind, and eager to provide a banquet feast for His people. But when people give Him the ultimate brush-off, when they turn their backs on heaven and say, "Sorry, not interested," that is a very serious thing. Especially when men and women pick up rocks or guns to drive away God's chosen prophet — or even just send him packing with words — that is a very serious thing. God certainly does want every citizen of this planet inside His banquet hall; the Bible says so many times. But it also teaches that those who blatantly and willfully defy this invitation and reject the messenger sent by the king will miss the wedding, the feast, and eventually life itself.

What happens next? The king throws open the banquet doors of that Hyatt Hotel. "Go get anybody!" he says. "Anybody, anywhere. Go into the back alleys. Go into the bars. Go into the brothels. Go from door to door, finding sick people, poor people, good people, bad people. Losers and lonely people. Go find the people who haven't darkened the door of a church in the last thirty years, but just once in a while listen to the *Voice of Prophecy* on the radio."

This king cranks up his printing press and engraves invitations with everyone's names on them. You get one; I get one. Our neighbors get them. The postman delivering them to our front doors gets one himself.

Maybe you've always been outside the hotel looking in as well-dressed couples went in. And you could hear the faint sounds of the orchestra, and just barely smell the hot buttered rolls, the salads, the desserts. But you never thought God's invitation was for you. Preachers get invited. People like Martin Luther and Billy Graham and the pope have an invitation. But not you.
Until right now. In fact, you're the guest of honor.

7

A PARTY AT 3:30 AM

So after the religious establishment and the ritzy and the rich and the royal have all turned down a free wedding invitation from their king, His Majesty opens up the banquet hall to everybody in town! Here's the CNN proclamation from verses 8 and 9: "'The wedding banquet is ready, but those I invited did not deserve to come. Go to the street corners and invite to the banquet anyone you find.' So the servants went out into the streets and gathered all the people they could find, both good and bad, and the wedding hall was filled with guests."

You've heard the expression: "a blanket invitation." Well, here's the world's greatest example of exactly that. Because God's got the biggest blanket of anyone in town. "Go get anybody," says the king. "I don't care who. Knock on doors everywhere. Get the street people. Get the gang members. Get the pool sharks and the hookers and the hustlers. My Son's getting married, and I need a full banquet hall."

If you've ever felt left out, that feeling should end right here in verse 9. Because God sends out His limousines and His uniformed ambassadors to bring an invitation right to your door. It's an urgent invitation, because the feast is about to begin. The band is about to play. And the king makes it perfectly clear that this invitation is sent out without regard to status or position or level of sinfulness or anything.

So that's the message of this chapter. God wants you! If you're reading this in prison, He wants you. If you're on Death Row, He wants you. If you're Mitchell Johnson and Andrew Golden, the two Arkansas schoolboys who murdered four students and a teacher early in 1998, He wants you. If you're in your car, in your house. If you're a runaway. If you're broke or if you're rich.

Right now He's saying to you, "I want you; you're invited to My Son's banquet feast."

I sometimes wish the *Voice of Prophecy* — especially these words right here — could air, not just on religious stations, but on all the hardest rock-and-roll stations too, the country stations, the heavy metal, rap, hip-hop, Top 40, dance, oldies, New Age, talk radio, sports . . . everything! Because this is the message that needs to go out to every single lonely person in the world. "You've been invited to a great banquet for the Son of God, Jesus Christ."

And let's talk about weddings for a moment. I guess at most functions like these, there are two kinds of guests: the casual drop-ins who don't really know the bride or the groom — and they sit in the back and get a free piece of wedding cake.

And then there are those who really are connected with the two newlyweds: they sit up close. They bring a nice gift. They wear their best clothes. But more than that, they love the bride and the groom. They're there to show support, to show that they are connected with these people. They identify with them. They support them. They truly are "well-wishers" in the best sense of the word. And when the preacher begins, "Dearly beloved, we are gathered together . . ." these are the people he's talking about. "Dearly beloved" people, friends and relatives, who dearly love the bride and the groom.

So you and I have been invited to a big wedding. Who's it for? The son of the king. Who is that? Well, it's Jesus, of course. Wouldn't you like to go to a banquet where our Friend Jesus is being honored? Furthermore, wouldn't you like to be one of those who sits down close to the front, as if to say, "Yes, I'm a close friend. I really do love the Groom! I support Him and have for a long time. This moment of victory for Him is one that thrills me too."

It's interesting and wonderful that God invites everyone, even strangers — especially strangers. But as we continue to study, we'll think about a man who came to the wedding, but didn't show much interest in ever identifying with the Groom. He was there with his own agenda, his own pride and motives. But God invites people to the wedding who really want to be the friend of the Groom, the Son of the King.

I think as we realize that, we can find more than one interpretation for what this wedding feast really is. True, it reminds us of the Second Coming of Jesus, when there will be a great feast in heaven. What a banquet that will be — and yes, every citizen of this world is now being invited to attend.

But in a larger sense, the wedding feast is an ongoing experience with the King and His Son even right now. Do you believe that? The invitation is out there now, and has been for 2,000 years. "Come in! Please come in! Wherever you are, whoever you are, come in and enjoy a relationship with the Groom; show your support for Him."

Again we peek ahead in the story and find that a man is eventually thrown out of this feast. Palace guards show him to the door, and we'll discuss the very sober reasons why that might happen. Of course, such an event would have to happen before the Second Coming of Jesus. Because in heaven, in God's kingdom where the real banquet begins, no one will ever leave or ever want to leave. All of the friends of the Groom will be eternally secure there.

There's a parallel story told by Jesus in Luke 14, and I don't intend to mix the two here. But in the second story, the invitation doesn't just go out to "everyone." Here the master specifies the following types of guests: "the poor, the crippled, the blind, and the lame." That's interesting, isn't it, and maybe from a spiritual perspective we find ourselves in one of those categories. Friend, are you poor? In your soul, is the bank account empty? Have you felt distant from God? Have you felt that Jesus was far from you and you from Him? Then this is good news, because God has invited you to His wedding feast.

Maybe you're blind — and of course, the book of Revelation tells us that we all have some cataracts when it comes to the things of God. But here God specifically wants to invite people who have been blinded to His goodness. "Maybe you don't trust Me yet," reads the invitation . . . perhaps written in Braille. Or coming in over the radio even. "Maybe you never glimpsed the wonder of Calvary, the personal gift I made for you. You're groping around in the darkness of discouragement or the confusion of drugs. That's all right; I don't hate you. I have an invitation for you instead."

Or you're crippled and lame. Crippled in terms of walking daily with Jesus. You haven't been doing it. Or you're emotionally crippled, too confused to really focus on the principles of God's kingdom. You read your Bible and it's a jumble, a confused mess to you. But right here God invites the cripples of the world to get into the limousine and ride directly over to the palace.

God longs for wedding guests who will become close friends of His Son. But He'll take us where we are right now! Because the wedding is right now! "Come this moment!" He says. "Dinner's about to be served. When you get here, I want you to meet My Son and learn to love Him, but first just come! Come just as you are."

In President Jimmy Carter's recent book, *Living Faith,* he relates an anecdote he heard from evangelist Tony Campolo. Tony was suffering from jet lag in Hawaii one night, and since he couldn't sleep, went to an all-night diner. Lo and behold, in the next booth over was a little group of prostitutes. Down on their luck — women who obviously were having a very hard life. And one of them said to the others, "You know, tomorrow's my birthday."

"Really?" And they teased her a bit. "How old are you going to be?"
"Thirty-nine." And then this lonely hooker added, "You know,
I've never once in my life had a birthday party."

Well, Tony Campolo filed that away. Later, when the girls were
gone, he got together with the manager of the diner, and arranged a
party for that lonely hooker, that prostitute. The next evening
when the same little group of "ladies of the evening" convened at
that diner, he sprang the surprise on the birthday girl. Cake, rib-
bons, presents, flowers, everything. He went all out with this surprise birthday party. All of the women were just blown away,
absolutely stunned and thrilled, of course, and Tony even had the
opportunity to pray with all of them, especially that lonely 39-year-
old hooker. Who knows? Maybe in his prayer, he was able to
mention a loving God in heaven who was about to throw a surprise
wedding banquet party of His own too.

But later, after all the cake was gone, and the girls were gone, and
they were cleaning up, the owner of the diner said to Tony: "Man,
what kind of church do you belong to anyway?" And Campolo
looked at him and said very quietly: "I belong to the kind of
church that throws birthday parties for whores at three-thirty in the
morning." And Jimmy Carter adds: "This was Jesus' kind of
church."

8
DESIGNER GOWNS FOR EVERYONE

If you didn't see *It's a Wonderful Life* on TV this past December, maybe you remember how a young idealist named George Bailey was the spiritual core of Bedford Falls. When the corrupt banker, Mr. Potter, tried to take over the Savings and Loan, it was George who singlehandedly saved the situation.

There was a run on the bank that day, and people were crowding around, demanding to get their money out. Old Potter was offering 50 cents on the dollar for anyone's shares, and a very earnest Jimmy Stewart had to try to keep people from selling out to the evil empire. And so he stands there, just minutes away from leaving on his long-awaited honeymoon. And he's got two thousand dollars — his own money. His honeymoon money. But one by one, he says to his friends, "How much do you really need to tide you over? What could you make do on?" And twenty dollars at a time, he gives out his own money to all of these clamoring people, hoping to keep them afloat, keep their hopes and dreams alive.

Well, the story of God's great banquet is kind of a wedding moment as well. There's a bridegroom, of course, and that's the king's own son. In other words, Jesus Christ. And so far we've been rejoicing over the fact that the invitation goes out to every person everywhere: in the highways and byways, to every corner of the globe.

And now comes the George Bailey moment from *It's a Wonderful Life*. Actually, there are two such moments. First of all, an invitation is issued . . . and how much does it cost the recipients? Every four years in the United States as candidates are lining up to be elected or re-elected, many people will put on their mink coats and their cummerbunds and attend $1000-a-plate fundraising dinners. But here in Matthew 22, the greatest banquet ever, there's no mention of a ticket price. In fact, it's very obvious — considering the ragtag clientele, the scandalous guest list — that this banquet is free. The king is simply throwing open the front doors and inviting everyone. "No charge! No two-drink minimum! No campaign pledges required!" All the riffraff of the world can simply walk into the chandeliered ballroom, sit down at a table with a damask tablecloth and candelabra, and be waited on by a maitre'd in a Pierre Cardin tuxedo.

Now, why does the invitation come to us free? Nothing in life is free, and if there's a banquet in a ballroom, there surely is a bill which is presented to someone, and there is a person somewhere who pays it. And never has that been so true as in this story. The price of this banquet was paid on Calvary. It was paid in full at the cross. Without the sacrifice of Jesus Christ on that Friday afternoon, without that greatest of ATM card swipes, God could not, would not, should not be able to morally let sinners into the great banquet hall of His kingdom. He couldn't do it! But this is the foundation message of the Christian faith — that our price of admission has already been paid. The Father and the Son themselves, the King and the Bridegroom in this story, pay the banquet charge for you and for me and for your neighbors and my neighbors. This is why the king can properly and justly say to His servants in verse 9: "Go to the street corners and invite to the banquet anyone you find."

Anyone! Anywhere! Good and bad alike. And there's no complaint from the hotel, because the price has already been paid for every place setting in the great hall. Jesus paid it all, and all to Him we owe. Just as George Bailey doled out money out of his own pocket, the Father sent us His beloved Son out of His own heart.

And it's so wrenching when people spurn this invitation. This "free" invitation which was actually so very, very expensive. It comes free to us, but it cost God everything. And what a poignant, terrible moment back in verse 5, where it says: "But they [the original guests] paid no attention and went off — one to his field, another to his business."

"Ho-hum," they said to one another. "Big deal, another banquet. It's free; how much can it be worth?" And they shrugged off the most important invitation of their very existences. The most precious piece of engraved paper the post office had ever delivered, and they sent it spinning into the trash can and surfed over to another TV show.

But now there's an important Part Two to this interesting story from our Lord. We now get to the part about the wedding garments, and our updated title for this parable: *I Can't Afford Your Free Tuxedo*. And maybe you've been wondering what that is all about.

The Scriptures don't explicitly state this, but many good Bible scholars have determined, or at least suggested, that in a story like this one, the king most likely provided not only free invitations, but also sent out at his own expense the proper attire for the gala occasion. In other words, everyone who got this royal invitation, whether rich or poor, high or low, good or bad, also was given a custom-fit tuxedo or a sequined gown by Halston, Versace, or Armani.

Especially if the king's ambassadors were looking for dinner guests on Skid Row and the bowery district, in trash dumpsters and crack houses, this would be a necessity. In the New International Version text notes the team of scholars makes this very suggestion: "It has been conjectured that it may have been the custom for the host to provide the guests with wedding garments. This would have been necessary for the guests at this banquet in particular, for they were brought in directly from the streets."

Now, all along, you and I have been deciding what this person represents and that one in this parable. That's part of the fun, part of the puzzle. But this point here is anything but light fun, because it's clear that this wedding garment, this tuxedo, is of vital importance. Having it on is so important that a man without it is shown to the fire exit and thrown back out into the street.

So we have to ask: what would be necessary for a person to enjoy fellowship with God forever at His wedding banquet? What does the Bible teach is the requirement or the standard to reach if a person wants to live in heaven?

That's not really hard to answer. All through the Old Testament and the New as well, we're taught that God is holy. He's righteous. He's sinless. In the Old Testament, the Ten Commandments describe the holiness and righteousness of God. In the Gospels, of course, we have the pure, sinless life of Jesus Christ. In the book of Romans, none other but Paul, the great preacher of the gospel of grace, tells us that our sins are what condemn us to death. That's Romans 6:23. So in order to be in this wedding banquet party, and especially in order to stay there, a person needs righteousness. He or she needs goodness. He or she needs a life of obedience.

Ah . . . and now the parable takes on a whole new light, an entirely different cast, with shades yet again of George Bailey and the gifts from his own wallet. Here's another word of explanation from the diligent Bible scholars for the NIV:

"The wedding garment no doubt speaks of the righteousness that God, the gracious host, provides for all who accept His invitation. God issues an undeserved invitation to undeserving people, and in addition provides the righteousness the invitation demands."

So we have here, not one, but two incredible gifts. First of all an invitation that's absolutely and completely and totally free. It is! There's no price tag on it anywhere except for the one already paid at Calvary.

And then since heaven is a place where righteous people only can dwell, this gracious King goes the necessary second step. He provides a robe of righteousness — a free tuxedo, an Armani gown — to every man or woman who wants to be a part of His wedding party. Now, whose righteousness is it in these tuxes and gowns? It's the righteousness of our Lord and Savior Jesus Christ. He lived a perfect life. He died on the cross to pay the price for all of those invitations. And then He and His Father grant to each one of us the opportunity to put on the second gift, the robe of His righteousness.

I have to ask: really, what more can any good host do? And all of us who stand in our new tuxedos and gowns in that resplendent banquet pavilion can only thank the King and say to each other: "It's a wonderful life!"

9
IS MR. T REALLY GOOD NOW?

This particular chapter first aired on our nationwide network of stations on a Thursday, May 21. And a couple of birthday names jumped out at us which had a kind of tie to this parable about a king who throws a free wedding banquet for all of the down-and-outers of the world.

It happened to be the 100th birthday (1998) of the great philanthropist Armand Hammer, who gave away millions of dollars to pet projects like cancer research and humanitarian aid to Russia. Also the anniversary of the 1991 death of Indian Prime Minister Rajiv Gandhi. He was killed by an exploding bomb hidden in a bouquet of flowers some seven years after his mother, Indira Gandhi, was also assassinated. And so we thought of how Jesus Christ was assassinated in order to pay the price for this great wedding feast.

Now, you're going to think this third birthday card is kind of odd . . . but the infamous Mr. T turned 46 years old on that day: May 21, 1998. Maybe you remember him starring in *The A Team*, or in WWF wrestling matches with his mohawk hair and tons of gold jewelry all over. Or maybe you recall the line he made famous in one of the Rocky movies where he vowed he would beat up on the Italian Stallion, Sylvester Stallone. "I pity the fool," he snarled — and it became his tag line. Why in the world would I mention a birthday bad boy like Mr. T? Well, stick around.

We're getting close, finally, to the finish line in this parable of Jesus, where a king sends out wedding invitations to all of the undeserving pond-scum-type people of the world. A free invitation, and then also a free wedding garment — a tuxedo or a designer gown — to wear to the big event. And right here in the story, as Christians really try to determine biblically what this wedding robe truly is, a debate breaks out and also some great concern.

Here's why. Obviously that wedding garment represents righteousness. Holiness. Obedience. Purity. Commandment-keeping. And so it gets very disquieting when we get to the end of the story, and here's what happens beginning in verse 11: "But when the king came in [to the feast] to see the guests, he noticed a man there who was not wearing wedding clothes. 'Friend,' he asked, 'how did you get in here without wedding clothes?' The man was speechless."

And what happens next? This is very sobering. "Then the king told the attendants, 'Tie him hand and foot, and throw him outside, into the darkness, where there will be weeping and gnashing of teeth.' For many are invited, but few are chosen."

So we have a wedding that is free. Everyone is invited to attend with no up-front fee being charged. But once inside, this question is asked: have you got on the proper robe? Are you sufficiently dressed? Are you righteous? And a man who stands there speechless when that question is asked, is unceremoniously thrown outside to the wolves, where there is weeping and gnashing of teeth, and maybe even some hot flames.

And we head into a tunnel here of bad news — good news. Because Christians read this Bible story, and they get to this part where the King comes in to see the guests. In fact, He's almost inspecting them, it seems. This is a kind of judgment scene. "Who's got on a wedding garment, a robe of righteousness?" It's clear from this story that at least one stubborn — or maybe ignorant — attendee doesn't have on the tuxedo, and is thrown out. And so we begin to say, "Wait a minute. If this story is true, then my assurance of salvation is shaken and shattered. How can I know if the King won't approve of what *I'm* wearing either? I'm certainly not as righteous as some of the others in my church, not as well-dressed, character-wise, as they are. This is bad news!"

Well, it isn't bad news after all. Because as we already discovered, the King provides the robe! It's given out free! You receive one; I receive one. We all receive one. In one commentary the writers make this suggestion: "The wedding garment represents 'the righteousness of Christ.' Hence, the rejection of the garment represents the rejection of those traits of character that qualify men to become sons and daughters of God. Like the guests in the parable, we have nothing suitable of our own to wear. We are acceptable in the presence of the great God only when clad in the perfect righteousness of Jesus Christ by virtue of His merits."

So what sounded like bad news isn't bad news at all. Because when the King comes in to see His guests, and when He comes by your banquet table, where the white linen is so sparkling white and the candles are twinkling in the darkness, and His eyes fall on you, what does He see? He sees the robe of Christ's perfect righteousness covering your sins. You appear in His eyes just as His own Son, Jesus, does. Perfect. Sinless. Loyal. Loving. Obedient. He looks at you and He sees Jesus' heart, Jesus' holiness. And He says, "Welcome to the feast for My Son. In fact, you look a lot like Him. I'm so glad you're here."

Back for a moment to big, bad, enemy-stomping Mr. T, and his birthday. Los Angeles Times columnist Mike Downey tells us something that maybe we didn't know. Mr. T, it's been reported, has cancer. What's more, he's a born-again Christian. Along with the chemotherapy for skin cancer, he has on the robe of Jesus' righteousness at this very moment. He tells what happened when he heard the bad news:

"I got down on my knees to pray. I said, 'Lord, give me the strength that You gave Abraham, that You gave Joseph, that You gave Moses, that You gave Job. Because how would I know that my God is a healer, if I never got sick. My God would be a fair-weather God if He was only with me when I got millions of dollars from doing *The A-Team* and commercials and whatnot. I don't want no fair-weather God. I want a God who will be with me through *everything.*"

That's the testimony of Mr. T. He doesn't want to be covered by boxing trunks or by all his gold necklaces or his mohawk. He wants to be covered by the robe of Jesus' righteousness.
But now what seems to be good news — the very best, in fact — takes us into another area of deep Christian debate. We wear this robe of Christ's righteousness. It's beautiful; it's free. We join Mr. T in thanking God for such a wonderful free tuxedo or evening gown.

But now the disturbing question. Is this robe simply and exclusively the righteousness and goodness and holiness of Jesus Christ which covers over our wickedness? Or is this robe a kind of righteousness which Christ gives to us . . . to the point where we ourselves are good and holy? Does He in fact come in and actually make His people good?

Or put it this way. Will heaven's banquet hall be inhabited by people who are forever wicked and sin-stained, but only covered up by someone else's million-dollar tuxedo? Some theologians refer to this as "legal fiction," where the whole universe has to forever pretend that bad people are good. Other Bible scholars debate about whether the holy character of Jesus is "imputed" to believers — in other words, simply credited to us in a mathematical sense — or "imparted" to us, where His goodness is in reality given to His people, and they actually become people who love righteousness.

Well, it's a big question, and that makes this a bad point for a chapter break. But you can see how a person's insecurities might come surging back. If this robe of righteousness has to in any way be my own goodness, then I begin to worry. Because maybe I don't see much progress in that department . . . and I hear the trumpet sounding as the great King of the universe begins to wind His way through the banquet pavilion, about to inspect the wardrobes of His guests.

But just a closing word — and again you and I turn to the Mohawk-haired Mr. T. This snarling, scowling, "I pity the fool" sneering, bad boy of wrestling and television. Now he's a Christian. Now he's got the robe of Jesus covering him. But lo and behold, something has actually happened to this man inside. That robe he is wearing has actually become HIM. He is now loving and tender, soft-spoken and kind. And he tells Downey how he now spends his time in children's cancer wards, quoting the Bible to them, visiting with kids for hours. He talks about his mother, how she raised him and his eleven siblings. His dad was a junkman who preached on Sundays.

"We were poor financially," he said, "but we were rich spiritually. Drugs and crime were all over me, under me and around me, but never in me. Why? Because I respected my mother. I'm a big, overgrown mama's boy. That's the problem with society. We don't have enough mama's boys. If we had more mama's boys, there wouldn't be so much disrespect for women."

And Downey said to him, "It must have been hard telling your mom about your cancer." And here's the end of the column: "And for the next few minutes in the restaurant, without a word, the biggest, strongest, roughest, toughest, baddest dude you'd ever want to meet is crying his eyes out, while I hold his hand. You would want to meet him, believe me. I pity the fool who never gets the chance."

Happy birthday, Mr. T. A son of God.

10
HAPPY WITH OUR OWN CLOTHES

Every Memorial Day here in the United States — and most countries have similar celebrations — there's a very plain truth we all have to face up to. Here it is: you and I are alive and well and free today because someone else died for us. The reason we don't live under the terrors of the Nazi swastika is because someone else died for us during World War II. The only reason we don't have a fragmented, broken-up U.S.A. is because soldiers died for us in the Civil War. Soldiers died to get that Berlin Wall down; they died for us in Vietnam. They've died for us in the Persian Gulf. And so, at least once a year, we pause to remember all of the brave, selfless people who have given their lives in combat for you and for me and for all of us who are living.

It's a bit hypothetical, but I guess it would be possible to turn down that gift. "No," we say. "Don't die for me. I don't accept that. My pride, or my stubbornness, or my streak of do-it-for-myself won't permit it. I'll earn my own liberty." And we march in a protest parade instead on the other side of Lafayette Park.

In this great parable, the price of the banquet has already been paid. Someone else already died to pay the way for each of us. The cross of Jesus is our own Memorial Day reminder, isn't it? But now our attention turns to the wedding robe also provided by the king. He mailed out to every would-be attendee a brand new, custom-fitted tuxedo or $2000 wedding dress from the designers in Paris. And that wedding gown is the righteousness of Jesus Christ. To be in the wedding hall, and in order to remain there in the presence of the king, every person in attendance absolutely must have on this robe of Christ's righteousness. In the Matthew 22 story told by Jesus, there was one man who, for whatever reason, had disdained the elegant wedding robe provided to him. "I don't need it," he must have said to himself. "What I've got on is fine." And he went in the front door wearing his own clothes, and soon found himself out in the back alleyway with the trash dumpsters and the empty soda cans and the rats and maybe even the hotel incinerator . . . if you take my meaning.

But now this debate point. Is this wedding robe, which we know is the righteousness of Jesus Christ, something that simply covers up our badness? Or is this robe a righteousness which Jesus actually gives us, and which honestly transforms us, makes us good and holy like Him? If it's the former, you would wonder why anyone would ever reject it? If it's the latter, if this robe is righteousness and holiness which actually gets inside of us and makes us Christlike, then many believers begin to worry and doubt and fret, because that doesn't seem to be happening very quickly in their lives. What if the King throws them out too? So this parable raises an important and practical question: is this robe of Jesus something which covers up our wickedness, or is it a garment which actually makes us good?

Do you know something? I'd like to suggest that the answer is yes! Yes to both questions! Yes, the robe of Jesus is a pure and spotless garment which covers up our great sinfulness. It qualifies us for heaven because of Calvary. And yes, the robe of Jesus' righteousness is a miraculous gift which also gets inside a person and touches the heart. Just like a tuxedo on a homeless person or a vagrant bum seems to bring out that person's best qualities, the wedding robe in this story is Christ reaching down into our hearts and making us really good, truly good from the inside out. It is not "legal fiction" where the whole universe has to forever pretend that wicked people are really okay after all.

So may I suggest to you that the wedding garment is both? Furthermore — and this point is extremely important — in both interpretations the robe is a gift from God. As the robe covers us, that is God's gift. And the robe transforms us, that robe is a gift too. Here's Ezekiel 36:24, which demonstrates the internal working of this wedding present: "I will give you a new heart and put a new spirit in you; I will remove from you your heart of stone and give you a heart of flesh."

Jesus, speaking to His disciples in John chapter 14, encouraged them with this motivation: "If you love Me, keep My commandments."

Paul, writing about the inner workings of this wonderful gift robe, says this in Romans 12: "Do not conform any longer to the pattern of the world, but be transformed by the renewing of your mind." And he goes on to emphasize the gift aspect of the robe, with this powerful promise in Philippians chapter 2: "It is God who works in you to will and to act according to His good purpose."

What an incredible gift this robe is! It's free on both counts, as it covers and as it transforms. This amazing, generous King really does it all, doesn't He? I like a quote from C. S. Lewis, in *Mere Christianity*, where he says this: "After the first few steps in the Christian life we realize that everything which really needs to be done in our souls can only be done by God."

He goes on to say a word of encouragement for any person who may worry that this gift robe isn't doing what it's supposed to do — that it's covering, but not transforming. Notice, and ironically, this is from a chapter entitled "Counting the Cost":

"The practical upshot is this. On the one hand, God's demand for perfection need not discourage you in the least in your present attempts to be good, or even in your present failures. Each time you fall He will pick you up again. And He knows perfectly well that your own efforts are never going to bring you anywhere near perfection. On the other hand, you must realize from the outset that the goal towards which He is beginning to guide you is absolute perfection; and no power in the whole universe, except you yourself, can prevent Him from taking you to that goal. That is what you are in for."

But what about the person who looks at himself in the mirror — without the robe of Christ — and says, "I think I'm all right as is. I look okay. I'm dressed for the feast with my own wardrobe"? The same book has a word of warning there as well:

"If you are a nice person — if virtue comes easily to you — beware! . . . If you mistake for your own merits what are really God's gifts to you through nature, and if you are contented with simply being nice, you are still a rebel: and all those gifts will only make your fall more terrible, your corruption more complicated, your bad example more disastrous. The Devil was an archangel once; his natural gifts were as far above yours as yours are above those of a chimpanzee."

Here at the Voice of Prophecy, we received a letter from a woman who'd had ties to this radio ministry for quite a while. This letter described her spiritual journey, which was very interesting. But then she suddenly made the statement that at the present time she was living a life that was free from sin. She was no longer sinning, she wrote. Now, to be honest, in the very same paragraph she did say that God had given her this gift. And she listed several sins that she simply does not commit — not once in a while, not ever.

Soon she felt led — by God, she wrote — to leave her church. Now she only kept company with others like her who were having the experience of living a life completely free from sin. "Why should I associate," she asked, "with people making twenty grand a year when I can be in the million-dollar club?" Because as she looked at herself, she truly felt that she had attained perfection.

Now let me be careful here in concluding. Because God *promises* to give us the gift of Christ's righteousness. That's biblical truth. But when a person looks into his or her own soul, and sees perfection there, what a temptation it might be to go to the wedding feast "wearing your own clothes." And so many of us in the church have to fight the temptation every single day of our lives . . . of thinking our own wardrobe is good. This foolish man in Matthew 22 must have thought that. "I worked hard for these clothes," he said. "I've obeyed God my whole life. Why should I accept this gift outfit, which is the same as admitting I'm a naked wretch on my own? I won't do it."

In a way, that's like celebrating Memorial Day without wanting any connection with the sacrifice that made it possible. "Give me my barbecue and my swimming pool and my TV with the ball games. Give me the shopping malls and the Internet and the goodies of the American lifestyle. But I don't want to acknowledge my debt to the man who bled and died. I don't need him; I don't want him." And the Christian who says, "I don't really need the Son and His robe. But I do want the free banquet."

How's it going to be with us? Pastor Morris Venden, in his classic "wedding garment" sermon, puts these two wedding R.S.V.P.'s in front of us. One: "I pray Thee, let me be excused." That's what the majority will say.

Or how about this one: "To the King of kings and Lord of lords: I have just received Your Majesty's urgent invitation to be present at the marriage supper of Your only-begotten Son. I hasten to reply. By Your grace, I'll be there. P.S. And thank You for the beautiful robe."

Year-End Report of the Ten Mutual Funds

11
PASSING "GO" AND GETTING $200

I've noticed recently that they've come out with some new editions of Monopoly, where the streets aren't the familiar Marvin Gardens and Boardwalk, out of Atlantic City, of course. There's a Los Angeles version now, with Sunset Boulevard and some of those streets. And even a Hollywood version, which I imagine has Rodeo Drive and all of the Beverly Hills boulevards featured in the high-rent district. It was amusing recently to read how comedian Steven Wright had made the comment: "I don't think it's right that only one company gets to make the game Monopoly!"

In any case, there's a common motif for many of these board games. Every player starts out with a certain amount of money, and the object is to make a lot more. As we all know, the goal in Monopoly is to not only have all the money for yourself, but to wipe out everyone else so that they don't have any. When every-one declares Chapter 11 except you, then you win.

Here in Matthew chapter 25 a kind of Monopoly game is being started, but with one huge difference. There are three players, and the master of the house sets them each up with an initial fund and instructs them to see what they could do with the money. Let's pick up the story right here in verse 14: "[The kingdom of heaven] will be like a man going on a journey, who called his servants and entrusted his property to them. To one he gave five talents of money, to another two talents, and to another one talent, each according to his ability. Then he went on his journey."

It's been a common theme in these parables thus far that the math of God's kingdom is poles apart from what we ever learned in grade school, or what you find printed inside the box of a Parker Brothers game. Because in this experiment, the master of the estate gives each of the men different amounts. When they pass "GO," they don't all collect $200; in fact, one man — apparently the smartest of the three — starts the game with five times as much as the low man on the totem pole.

Now, the Bible tells us why the master does this. Notice: he gave them talents "each according to his ability." The man with the greatest potential got the most, and the servant with very limited investment skills got a rather small portfolio.

And how do we as humans feel about this kind of skewed, biased math? As we first recorded this radio series, here in Los Angeles, the 1998 baseball season was just getting underway. And Mike Piazza, the catcher for the Dodgers — admittedly the best player on the team, and maybe for the whole franchise in quite a few years — had been holding out for a new contract. He wanted something like a hundred million dollars over the next seven years. A hundred million dollars! Many, many other players — all of them, in fact — were getting quite a bit less than that. A few of them have to scrape by almost on welfare, earning maybe only a couple hundred thousand dollars a year.

And those of us sitting in the stands, way up high in the red seats, just can't relate at all to these kinds of home run numbers. But here's a man who wanted to be paid "according to his abilities." (As stunned fans around the world know, the new top brass in Dodgerland traded him away instead!) But in the Bible, this master or team owner, who represents God, actually does hand out different sums to different people based on HIS assessment of abilities.

If we segue from thinking of "talents" as money, to thinking of "talents" as abilities or . . . *talents*, of course, that's the point of this whole story. And anytime you go to a church and sit down in a pew, you're immediately confronted with this. Some Christians just plain and simple have more abilities than other ones. Some preachers are better than others. Some believers barely have one gift, if that, while others seem to do absolutely everything in the church, do it well, and drive up to the church parking lot in a Rolls

Royce to boot. And they're the people, obviously, who started out the game with the five thousand dollars.

The thing we all have to keep in mind every day of our lives, of course, is this: whose money is it? It belongs to the master, doesn't it? It wasn't the servants' money; it was the boss's. He entrusted it to them, but it was still his. And so it was entirely appropriate for him to look real hard at the resumés of his servants, and then place them in charge of different money market accounts according to his own wisdom about what they could handle.

Now, how is it when it comes to the Christian man or woman and the issue of talents? Whose talents are they? Well, maybe you think that your abilities are your abilities, but think again. Where'd they come from? Who gave them to you? Who entrusted you with the talents you have today, right now?

In the *Tyndale New Testament Commentary* for Matthew written by Dr. R. T. France, the author makes this comment: "In the context of Jesus' ministry the sums of money entrusted to the slaves are more likely to represent not natural endowments given to men in general, but the specific privileges and opportunities of the king-dom of heaven."

You see, you might be good with your hands. Or you might have a great singing voice, or be skilled at organizational matters. Those are your gifts — and to be sure, they came to you from God. But in the Christian faith, it's also true that when a person commits his or her life to God, they're also endowed with spiritual gifts that go beyond just talents and musical aptitude. Leadership turns into *spiritual* leadership; a hospitable personality is especially guided into the spiritual gift of giving a person spiritual comfort. And here for sure, we can know that the gifts are God's ownership, and that they're simply entrusted to us for use in service to Him.

In the telling of this little story, Jesus gives us a clue as to the importance of these talents. In Bible times, we read in various commentaries, a talent of silver was a huge amount of money. A talent was equivalent to 60 "minas," and a mina was a hundred drachmas. Well, that doesn't mean much until we learn that a drachma was basically a day's pay for the common person. That would make a talent — just one talent — the equivalent of six thousand days' pay. That's about twenty years' worth of salary for most of us, and this master gives out five talents, two talents, and one talent to these three men. So it's not just pocket change; this is a serious expression of trust and also a great spiritual challenge. "What will you do with this money?"

But I want to reiterate again: this is God's money. Or in your case, these are the talents God entrusted to you or loaned to you. That line got a bad rap a few years ago when a certain Rush Limbaugh liked to boast on TV that he was "talent on loan from God." But in the best of senses (and humblest too) that's a true statement. Our money and our fortunes and our abilities are really God's resources entrusted to us.

This should give each of us two things for sure. One would be a quiet combination of humility and contentment. If you're a genius, it's because that's what God gave you. If you're a millionaire, that's God's blessings. True, you may have worked hard to use and fine-tune those gifts and turned them into a nice fortune. But who gave you the aptitude to be a hard worker, a success-minded person instead of a sleep-in-till-noon bum? That came from God too.

So as we consider this human package called SELF, and then as we look around at the other packages in the house or in the church — some of them bigger and better, some of them not quite as good — can we be content and humble because this is how God gave things out? That's so hard to do, isn't it? And don't we all spend a lot of time each day either complaining to God that we're on the short end, or patting ourselves on the back for being somewhere on the rich-and-pretty end of the spectrum?

And point two is this: if the money is God's, then shouldn't we be bold in investing for Him? He told us to go for it! He challenged us to double His portfolio! He went on an important trip and left us in charge of some pretty exciting missions down here! Are we taking a chance, investing here, looking over there for the best and brightest opportunities? Sometimes people bet scared with their own little bankroll, but God has invited us to do great things with the talents He loaned us. He wants two to turn into four, and five to turn into ten . . . and then twenty, and forty, and so on. It's His money; it's His game; in fact, it's His Wall Street.

12
AFRAID TO PLAY THE GAME

Just a few years back there was a little fund of money at our Adventist Media Center that needed to be invested somehow. Just a few thousand dollars. It wasn't tagged for immediate operations, and so our treasurers needed to sort out the options and decide what to do.

Well, there were CDs, of course, and bank accounts and bond accounts and no-load mutual funds and all the rest. There also at this time were individual stocks too, naturally. And one in particular seemed to hold real potential, but as the decision-makers looked real hard at their options, they just couldn't see taking the risk. This certain company — and of course, I couldn't tell you the name of it, but it starts with "M" and is based up in the Pacific Northwest and has to do with computers and that's really all I can say — was just too much of a gamble.

Well, a few years have gone by, and that money made a little bit of interest. But if it had been put into that certain "M" company that specializes in software, the fund would have been worth a cool million dollars by now. And I guess we all know stories like that one.

Including this story in the Word of God! Even Jesus seemed to know about the bull market of the 1990s and He tells this story in Matthew chapter 25 of three fund managers who were given quite a pot of cash to play with while he was overseas checking out some hot tips and derivative deals in the Pacific Rim market.

Well, how did the three entrepreneurs do? The market was hot at the time, apparently, and trading was fast and furious in the pit. Let's pick up the story in verse 16: "The man who had received the five talents went at once and put his money to work and gained five more. So also, the one with the two talents gained two more."

There's an intriguing little "Greek nuance" hiding right here, and if you never noticed it before, well, neither did I. But in the King James Version, verse 15 sets up the story this way: "[He gave] to every man according to his several ability; and straightway took his journey."

Now here's the bit of trivia. The scholars question now if maybe that word "straightway" might actually belong to verse 16, not verse 15. So that instead of the master going "straightway" — or right away — on his journey, that word really applies to the first servant. So that this man who was entrusted with five talents got to work "straightway," or immediately, and got started just as soon as he could in the investing.

And you know, I like that enthusiasm! Right away this man wants to score a victory for his Lord. He knows this is a huge sum of money, many years' worth of salary. And so he doesn't say, "I'll get started first thing tomorrow." No, he begins making phone calls immediately; he calls the overseas markets; he rushes down to the corner and gets a copy of the Wall Street Journal. What are the rates right now? Are pork belly futures the thing to buy? (Actually, considering the players in this story, that probably wasn't his first choice.) But this first servant had a sense of urgency about him; he wanted to get that money working right away.

I had a sorry little experience when my wife Lisa and I bought a house recently. We were all set to close escrow on a Friday and move in that same day. But somebody slipped up and just one little document didn't get signed and notarized right. No big deal, right? Well, it turned out to hurt quite a little bit because the loan didn't fund that Friday; it held over until the following Monday. And that wouldn't seem so bothersome either, except for the fact that since we had moved in on Friday, the builder now wanted three full days of RENT! . . . enough to make up for the fact that he didn't have the money-making power of those loan funds for just those three days. A hundred and fifty extra dollars just out of the blue, because money didn't get "into the game" on Friday. Ouch ouch ouch!

But we can learn a lesson here. God has given each of us gifts . . . and the stakes are high! Those gifts you have, whatever they are, need to get "into play" right away. That's one of the biblical lessons of this story. Whether it's financial blessings or the gift of witnessing or the ability to make friends and lead them to Christ or the talent for showing hospitality for people less fortunate, the time to begin investing is now. Immediately. In all my years of involvement with local churches — and of course, I have to lecture myself too on this same point — it was so painfully obvious how the Church, the Body of Christ, was often held back because spiritual gifts were buried in the ground. People had talents, and they simply were not being used. And again I say, sometimes it's been me. "I'll get started with this later," I say to myself. "I know I *could* do that, and I *should*. But not right now. Maybe when summer's over." And a whole six months of investing opportunity for the Lord is wasted.

As we return to the story, notice that one servant decides to just not get into the game at all. Verse 18: "But the man who had received the one talent went off, dug a hole in the ground and hid his master's money."

Well, that's been a very convenient "attack line" ever since! "Burying your talent in the ground." Right here is where that expression comes from. And when you think of it, all of the "buried treasure" stories in the world and *Raiders of the Lost Ark* trilogies do have this stigma of waste. Resources that could have been in the game, in the market, building a future with the miracle of compound interest . . . but instead they're buried under a rock someplace or in an ancient tomb in Tibet.

And so we ask "Why?" Why did this man not get in the game? When these messages aired on the radio, I used as a promo line this excuse: "Well, the Dow Jones was due for a crash, and the bond market is wobbly right now. And banks are only paying 1.78% with a puny deposit like this. So I cashed out your funds and kept the money in my sock drawer. Here."

So that could be one reason: the element of risk. The Dow Jones is sky high, and what goes up has to eventually come down, we think. And so we don't invest.

From a spiritual point of view, are there elements of risk to investing our God-given talents? Sure there are! Someone gets a call to the mission field, and right away people point out nine hundred bad things that can happen. A would-be preacher thinks about the cost of going to seminary. Then what if he doesn't get a call? What if he and his family can't make it on a minister's salary? What if the congregation rejects him? Believe me, there are a million reasons to stay in a poolside lounge chair instead of getting into the water.

The element of risk might also be linked with our feelings about the fact that other people got the big pile of talents while we only got one. And face it, people all around us are rolling in talents. Which makes it seem all the more dangerous if we timidly raise our hands and volunteer with our one little gift. What if people sniff at the very suggestion? What if we get the famous "Don't call us; we'll call you"? And perhaps there's a bit of pouting as we go out back with our little shovel to bury our pitiful little stash.

But probably the biggest reason for the hole-in-the-ground strategy is recorded right here in the Bible. I'm skipping ahead in the story, but here's the excuse given by Contestant #3: "'Master,' he said, 'I knew that you are a hard man, harvesting where you have not sown and gathering where you have not scattered seed. So I was afraid and went out and hid your talent in the ground. See, here is what belongs to you.'"

You know, this pathetic speech reveals two enormous misunder-standings on the part of this man. First of all, he doesn't really understand whose money it is, and tragically, he especially doesn't understand the master himself. The Living Bible adds this insight to the speech: "Sir, I knew you were a hard man, and I was afraid you would rob me of what I earned, so I hid your money in the earth."

This servant gives himself away, doesn't he? First of all, he thinks the master is a hard man. Sure, he works for the boss and accepts a paycheck. But he doesn't like him, doesn't trust him. He's seething with resentment, especially over the fact that he's the last man in the five-and-two-and-one scheme. And so he says: "You're a hard man; you expect to score off other people's work."

And then this last giveaway line: "I was afraid you would rob ME of what I earned." I ask again: Whose money is this? Whose talents are these which are entrusted to the men? It's not their talents; it's the master's money! The original investment is his, and so the profits are his as well.

Right now, why not think about your best talent? Actually, God's talent or gift which is on loan to you. Right? It's His, not yours. He takes the risk, not you. And yet He invites you and me both to the victory party when the dividends roll in. Now, isn't that actual-ly a pretty good Boss to work for?

13
"PLEASE PASS ME YOUR PIE"

It seems like about once a year now, a hot-selling writer named
Bob Woodward comes out with a new book. As half of the famous
Woodward and Bernstein team that broke the Watergate scandal,
he has a knack for getting the inside scoop, the hidden details that
escape the attention of others.

One of his books, entitled *The Choice*, chronicles the early parts of
the 1996 presidential race, right up to the point where the
Republicans chose Bob Dole and the Democrats, of course, stayed
with the Clinton-Gore ticket. How did Dole, at his age, manage to
fend off Lamar Alexander and Phil Gramm and Pat Buchanan and
Steve Forbes and all the others? What about the Colin Powell factor — why didn't he run? And he certainly has all the juicy
details on the Democrats as well.

And on that side of the aisle, a certain element was a rather key
factor. That certain element was the shadowy figure of Dick
Morris. Several years later now, most of America knows about his
own sex scandal and some of the sordid headlines from 1996. But
Woodward reveals how this political operative schemed and
worked to exert more and more and more influence on the
President of the United States. He formulated policy: what he
called the scheme of "triangulation." He established fund-raising
goals and plans. He faxed ideas up to the President when he was
35,000 feet up in the sky on Air Force One. He even wrote many
of Bill Clinton's speeches for him.

Well, you can understand that the rest of the White House staff
didn't think much of this steamrolling tank which was taking over
all of their jobs. So they quickly worked to minimize the influence
of Mr. Dick Morris, get him cut off from having close access to the
Oval Office. But this ambitious operative just kept on grabbing
turf for himself, carving away out of other people's pies. If an

agency got him officially banned, he quietly established what were called "back channels." He found ways to get his proposed TV spots and suggested "State of the Union" addresses smuggled into 1600 Pennsylvania Avenue and onto President Clinton's desk.

Now, is there anything wrong with such ambition? Here's a man who kind of wanted to rule the world, and he'd step on as many toes as he had to. And here's this Bible parable told by Jesus Christ, where a rich businessman gave trust sums to three of his associates, and then left them to their own devices. How would they do with their allotments of five million bucks, two million, and one? And in exploring what the Word of God says about the three men, we find the master congratulating the ambitious ones. Here's the verbatim transcript, recorded by the secret taping device in the Oval Office, maybe:

"After a long time the master of those servants returned and settled accounts with them. The man who had received the five talents brought the other five. 'Master,' he said, 'you entrusted me with five talents. See, I have gained five more.' His master replied, 'Well done, good and faithful servant! You have been faithful with a few things; I will put you in charge of many things. Come and share your master's happiness."

The exact same line is repeated with Investor #2. He'd doubled his portfolio as well, and received the same words of praise and commendation. "Well done, good and faithful servant! You have been faithful with a few things; I will put you in charge of many things. Come and share your master's happiness."

So are these two men a couple of first-century Dick Morrises? Aggressive, power-driven, back-biting and back-channeling, bruising egos in order to score big on the stock market? And is there anything wrong with wanting to enlarge your slice of the pie?

Well, there are several things we could say about that. First of all,

the Bible clearly teaches in this story that God Himself acknowledges and even intends the disparity of gifts in the Church. It was
God who gave out the five, the two, and the one talent in this story!
One Bible commentary shared this insight in discussing the
Matthew 25 parable: "The amount entrusted to each servant was no
more than, in the estimation of his master, he could handle wisely;
at the same time it was sufficient to challenge his ingenuity and
skill and thus provide him with an opportunity to gain experience."

So even in God's system of government, there's room for a man or
woman to rise up to become Secretary of State, or for a person to
hold down two cabinet posts, as Henry Kissinger used to do.
Some preachers are given authority over a huge conference or dio-
cese, while another man or woman has a little country church with
eighteen people in it. Both are precious to God, and both are
rewarded if they do their best with the circumstances and talents
entrusted to them. And certainly both are encouraged to seek more
influence and a wider scope of service if their motivation is right.

In his excellent book, *Surprised by the Power of the Spirit, Dr.*
Jack Deere shares four suggestions regarding the topic of spiritual
gifts or talents. First, we should pray for such gifts. The Bible
teaches that in First Corinthians 12. We should attempt to regular-
ly use the gifts that we do have. Of course, that's the very point
made in this parable of the three servants. If you have five, use
five. If you have two, use two. If you have one, for sure don't go
out in the woods and bury the one.

Third suggestion: we should study the gifts, the doctrine of spiritual gifts. We should study how to use our gifts more effectively. I
imagine the two good servants in this story pored over all kinds of
manuals and investment forms; they were on the Internet every
day, tracking the market, looking for tips. They got the Charles
Schwab Newsletter. They made themselves experts on fund man-
agement.

And then Deere's fourth suggestion: have friendships with people who are more advanced in the gifts than we are. Rub shoulders with others who are also active in working for God. Share strategies; exchange success stories; look for tips. Tell how God is blessing your efforts for Him.

But as Jack Deere makes all these suggestions, he firmly and emphatically takes all of us back to a core Bible text found here in First Corinthians 12:7: "Now to each one the manifestation of the Spirit is given for the common good."

Notice: "for the common good." Whatever successes come through our efforts are to be given to the Master's house. They're for the good of everyone. If one person doubles his money, everyone rejoices, because that's a success for the whole family. This is why the one servant was so wrong when he said to the boss: "I was afraid you'd rip off the profits I'D made."

And secondly, this tells us what kind of aggressiveness is appropriate as we seek to serve. Eagerness and ambition and zeal and horizon-expanding are all good traits, as long as we are serving the Master and His kingdom. As long as we are working for the common good. Even Dick Morris initiatives are all right as long as they are for the good and the uplifting of America and not just the good of Dick Morris.

Speaking of politics makes me think of another man who often sat in the Oval Office and sent faxes to many presidents. Billy Graham certainly has to be a man we would think belongs in the "five talent" club. Look how God has blessed him! Many talents were bestowed upon this Southern Baptist preacher, and God also allowed many breaks to come his direction.

And he has been ambitious in his career. It takes a bit of boldness to start a huge soulwinning team and then allow it to have this name: the BGEA — Billy Graham Evangelistic Association.

Without a doubt, there have been those who criticized the size and scope of his operations, suggesting that he had too much power and influence in God's kitchen cabinet.

And yet here's a line from the very first page of the preface to his autobiography, *Just As I Am:* "If anything has been accomplished through my life, it has been solely God's doing, not mine, and He — not I — must get the credit."

In fact, on the jacket cover of his book comes this additional disclaimer: "I have often said that the first thing I am going to do when I get to Heaven is to ask, 'Why me, Lord? Why did You choose a farmboy from North Carolina to preach to so many people, to have such a wonderful team of associates, and to have a part in what You were doing in the latter half of the twentieth century?'" And then he confesses: "I have thought about that question a great deal, but I know also that only God knows the answer."

Maybe you look up at heaven every night too, and say "Why me?" Or maybe you're looking up there and saying to God, "Why NOT me?" That's okay. As long as our ambitions and our steps up the success ladder are motivated by a desire to lift Jesus higher and not ourselves.

Happy climbing.

14
THE RADIO SCRIPTWRITER WHO NEVER ONCE, A SINGLE TIME IN HIS LIFE, HIT A HOLE-IN-ONE

Under the category of "unfair unfair unfair" there sure are a lot of stories that rub the fur the wrong way. Why is it that the rich get richer and the poor get poorer? I already mentioned Mr. Michael Piazza, the ballplayer who was publicly angling for a long, multi-year $100 million contract. And his comments about it ended up in most of the newspapers around L.A., causing him to be booed rather roundly whenever he came up to the plate.

But here's the irony: this young man was born into wealth already! His father is a very successful businessman back east, and this baseball catcher was born into millions before his home-run power made him a candidate for even more money.

Every now and then there's a story in the paper about a person who hits the lotto jackpot TWICE! I mean, the big prize. And why? Why does God let that happen? They don't need the money. But here they win $25 million or so the first time around, and then later they match all six numbers a second time.

Just a few weeks ago, a 49-year-old lady named Jeanette Roberts didn't just shoot a hole in one in golf . . . she hit three of them in the space of eight days! She'd only been playing the game for four years, compared to several sorry lifetimes for some of the rest of us. She's a 35-handicap, which is nothing to write home about. In fact, her scores on the three rounds where she hit these aces were as follows: 101, 91, and another 101. But there in those sky-high scores were three shots that just rolled right onto the green and went *plink* straight into the cup. To add insult to even more injury, these three fluke miracles are on top of a fourth hole-in-one that Jeanette had lucked out with earlier there at Granite Bay Country Club.

Well, like I say, the world isn't very fair. And as we read through
some of the stories that Jesus Christ told, it's clear that dealing
with the element of unfairness in the gospel message is kind of a
common theme. Prodigal sons get what they don't deserve.
People get invited to banquets they have no business attending.
And here in the parable of the three servants and the talents, there's
another occurrence of what we might call the bad math of the
kingdom.

By now the owner of the estate has heard glowing reports from
two of his financial lieutenants. The man with five talents earned
five more; the guy with two suitcases of money also doubled his
stake. And now comes Servant #3, the man who was only given
one measly talent. What kind of answer does he give when the
spotlight is shone on him? Here it is, beginning in verse 24:
"'Master,' he said, 'I knew that you are a hard man, harvesting
where you have not sown and gathering where you have not scattered seed. So I was afraid and went out and hid your talent in the
ground. See, here is what belongs to you.'"

Well, that's not too good, is it, especially considering that there
was a bull market going on and the other men in the game had
both had a return of 100%. So how does the boss respond to this
chicken-hearted guy?

"His master replied, 'You wicked, lazy servant! So you knew that
I harvest where I have not sown and gather where I have not scattered seed? Well then, you should have put my money on deposit
with the bankers, so that when I returned I would have received it
back with interest."

And now here's the kicker to the story, where the unfair math pops
up again: "Take the talent from him," [the master said], "and give
it to the one who has the ten talents. For everyone who has will be
given more, and he will have an abundance. And throw that
worthless servant outside, into the darkness, where there will

weeping and gnashing of teeth."

Isn't that quite a story? It's interesting that "gentle Jesus, meek and mild" seems to have quite a few anecdotes up His sleeve where someone is bodily tossed out into the darkness where the teeth begin to grind in sorrow. But even more important is the fact that the boss takes this one talent from the no-account man and hands it over to the person who's already prospering. Here in Matthew 25, the poor gets poorer and the rich gets richer and the player who's already gotten a hole in one gets three more in a week.

There's so much we could glean from this colorful story, but it certainly seems that the most important thing is to understand the Master! That's God, of course. Two of these servants seemed to know the Boss quite well. They enjoyed working for Him, didn't they? When He gave them a challenge, they got right to work. They invested with zest and enthusiasm. Interestingly, there seems to have been no resentment between them over the fact that one got five talents and the other only two. That's quite a spread, but they didn't mind because they knew and trusted the Master. It was His call; that was fine with them. They knew it was His money they were risking, but they also seemed to feel confident and secure that He would love them and accept them and be proud of them no matter how they scored in their stock market forays.

Here's another interesting note. How were these two good guys rewarded? Notice how the Master pays them: "Well done, good and faithful servant! You have been faithful with a few things; I will put you in charge of many things."

Did you pick that up? He says to them, "You men did good with a little bit of work. So your reward is . . . MORE work!" They went from a small amount of service to a large amount. Is that a reward? Is that a lovely payoff? Most of us, if we turn in a good job and meet a little deadline, aren't that thrilled when the big man in the corner office says to us, "Good job! Now here's a huge pile of work with even tighter deadlines!" And yet this is the reward for these two workers: increased responsibility.

But then this P.S.: "Come and share your Master's happiness!" Maybe you remember the King James spin given to that line: "Enter thou into the joy of thy lord."

Which follows the "more work" announcement: "I will make thee ruler over many things." Which, except for the politically minded among us, is usually not received as good news.

But for these two, it certainly was. They loved and appreciated this Master so much that to work for Him was a great reward. When He said to them, "I've got even bigger jobs for you now," that was by definition "entering into the joy of their Lord."

And of course, to understand this good Master helps render obsolete not only the "bad math" of the gospel, but the false charge of this wicked servant. It's interesting, by the way, that to do nothing with what God has given us is described by Jesus as not just laziness but downright wickedness and sin. That's something to think about, isn't it? But now let's examine this false accusation. Investor #3 says to the CEO, "Man, you're a hard boss. You expect to score every time, and off the sweat of others. You want to harvest where you didn't plant and gather where you didn't put in any seeds."

Well, if in this parable God is the Master, is that a true statement? When we do well for the kingdom, is God gaining a benefit that really didn't come from His original generosity? A missionary sweats in the jungle for years, and a few people are baptized in a little mountain stream; they become new Christians. Is God capitalizing on the hard work of that missionary, and getting a harvest where He didn't plant? Of course not! It was God who gave that native a conscience; it was God who softened his heart; the saving

Calvary message came from Him in the first place. Furthermore, it was God who gave the missionary the talents and the motivation and maybe even the finances to make that mission trek. It's a dynamic, living partnership, and I don't know of many missionaries who have ever come home complaining that God was a hard and unfair Boss. Most of them say it was the greatest reward of their lives to work for such a Master . . . and they thank God if He gives them ten cities to rule next time instead of only five.

And by the same token, there's no such thing as "bad gospel math" in God's vineyard. I've been in Russia where faithful Christians behind the forbidding Iron Curtain labored in secrecy for decades, with very sparse results. Then here comes a big American TV evangelist and he rents a huge Moscow Olympic stadium and has enormous crowds and baptizes 15,000 people. Do the workers there complain or do they celebrate? The ones I've met rejoice and consider that they are all full partners working for the same miracle-working Savior.

Here in the world of Christian radio there are many, many ministries bigger than the Voice of Prophecy. And I thank God if He pours on and piles on the blessings for someone who comes on after we do. If some other preacher on this dial already has ten talents, and then gets one more, we should praise the Lord, shouldn't we, that those funds are still invested in the same growing bull market.

You know, I think I'm going to stop saying "bad math." It's starting to add up better and better all the time.

15
ASK NOT WHAT HEAVEN CAN DO FOR YOU

It's probably the inaugural soundbite of all time — and I'm sure you've seen the black-and-white newsreel footage from Washington, D.C., going back to January 20, 1961. A young Massachusetts senator stood there in the wintry cold at the presidential microphone, where he had just accepted the mantle of leadership from Dwight D. Eisenhower. The torch had just been passed to a new generation, he announced. And then he said this: "And so, my fellow Americans, ask not what your country can do for you. Ask what you can do for your country."

The invitation to do something for a grand cause resonates powerfully with this Bible story of the talents. The owner of the estate gives three men a clarion call to do something for the kingdom. They're not investing for themselves; they're not using their own money and feathering their own nests — well, one of them was — they're in service to their Lord. They're doing His work; they're working for the success of His organization.

You know, all along it's been clear that God represents the landowner in this story. He's the One who knows His servants; He's the One who determines who will receive what talents and in what amounts. He's the One who issues the challenge and who provides the resources for this grand project. And of course, ultimately, we all report to Him because we're all in this story, aren't we? You've got a mutual fund to manage and so do I.

And yet it might be well here at the close to amend our story a bit, or perhaps to grow in our understanding. Is it possible that Jesus Himself — who is also God, to be sure — was representing Himself in this Matthew 25 parable? After all, in actual fact, He indeed did depart this world and return to heaven, leaving behind men and women with the assignment to work hard in His absence. That adds some real dynamic urgency to the story if you and I think of this Leader as being our own Savior. If it's Jesus who has placed these talents, these gifts, in your hands and in my hands, wouldn't we want to do our very best for Him? Remember again how two of these servants got to work "straightway," the old King James says. In other words, they eagerly got down to business. They must have admired and appreciated their boss very much to want to please him with a good report.

In verse 15, the Bible says rather cryptically: "Then [after giving out the talents] he went on his journey."

Then the thought is concluded in verse 19. "After a long time the master of those servants returned and settled accounts with them."

Well, a question comes to mind. How long is "a long time"? We don't know. For how many months or years was this master away? We don't know. Did he ever call in, or give them a beeper number? We don't know. Did he stay away longer than they expected? We don't know. It must not have been too many years, or the servants' achievement of doubling their money wouldn't be that impressive. But the Bible does say that it was a long AND unspecified time.

Now if we think of Jesus as being this Master, doesn't the parallel give us something to think about? He's been gone a long time, hasn't He? Far longer than most Christians ever thought it would be. My grandparents and great-grandparents were so sure they would live to see Him come back in the clouds. The early Christians were sure of it too. Something that the workers in the field were so positive would only be a few months or years or decades has now spread out to 2,000 years.

And so what's the lesson? Very simply this. The good servants just keep on working for their Master until He gets back. They don't get discouraged. They don't ever say, "Well, I've done enough" — and quit. They don't assume that the experiment has been canceled and cash in the funds for themselves. They simply keep on working with those talents, growing them, expanding them, adding to them. As long as there's breath in them to work, they work.

Which takes me right to the second conclusion. What would it feel like to meet Jesus on that great Homecoming Day and have to report that we did absolutely nothing with the gifts He gave us? In all that time. How would that feel? Can you imagine the tragedy of having to do that?

Now the thief on the cross came to the Lord at the last possible moment. But even he invested immediately in Jesus — confessing Him and them boldly shushing up his fellow inmate. He did what he could in those last few minutes of life. But you and I — we're here on a good playing field with a heaven-sent strategy and with talents in our possession. We don't have any excuse. And I ask again, while examining my own soul right here too — what would it feel like to face Jesus Christ, our wonderful, generous Savior, on that day, and have no report to give?

And He asks very gently: "I gave you 70 (or so) years of time. What did you do with it?" "Uh, nothing." "I gave you the ability to earn money. What'd you do with that?" "Uh, nothing there either, Lord." "I put neighbors on both sides of your house and across the street. Did you share with them, help them, lift them up, introduce them to Me?" "No, I guess I never did." "I invited you to walk with Me and experience obedience and character growth? Did you do that?" "No, I'm afraid I didn't do that either. I meant to, but . . ."

Can you imagine what a sad experience that would be? Not because Jesus is a harsh judge, a cruel boss with a miserly, forbidding scowl. But because He was so generous! "Ask not," He had said, "what the kingdom of heaven can do for you . . . although it's done so much. What can you do — what HAVE you done — for

My kingdom and My Father's kingdom?"

In *Parables of the Kingdom*, Morris Venden speaks of how we always compare who got what gifts, and how we were unfairly treated, and all the rest. But then he makes this conclusion: "The basic premise of the Christian religion is that all are workers. We may work in different ways, our talents may differ, but there is one common denominator. We will have something to tell about Jesus."

And maybe that's the one talent every single man and woman in the kingdom has been given. Others may have more, but we all do have that one gift: the ability to say something to someone about the wonderful Master we serve, our Friend Jesus Christ.

So let's ask ourselves this: have we been waiting on the sidelines? Have we invested zero so far? Have we dug a little hole in the dirt and put our gifts in there? Well, the good news is this: we can dig those talents up right now! Shovels can bury, but they can also dig up! We can start today. The investment game for Jesus Christ is still going on. Others may have already climbed higher than you, dreamed more and achieved more. But it's not too late for you to begin right now.

I've been reading lately about Australian beekeeper Edmund Hillary and Sherpa mountain climber Tenzing Norgay, who stood on the summit of Mount Everest on May 29, 1953. And of course, everyone talks about them being the first ones to the top. They got all the headlines; Sir Edmund Hillary even got knighted by a grateful British empire. In the intervening years, of course, some 700 others have made it to the top too. Others have died; still others have climbed partway — done their best.

And in the Christian expedition, it's not important who gets there first, or who climbs how high. That's not the issue; God says it's not the issue. Our heavenly Father invites us to simply climb with

the talents He's given us, the ropes with which He's secured us, the
climbing partners He's teamed us with. The success of the mission
is His responsibility; He leads the way.

And what's at the finish? I did a little bit of Bible math and figured out that even the man with just one talent had been given 20
years' salary to invest. It actually was a whole lot of money! And
then notice how God, the grateful owner, says to the good workers:
"Well done, good and faithful servant. You have been faithful with
small things. Now I have some big things for you!" And we think
to ourselves: *small*? An amount equal to 6,000 days' salary is
small?

Well, if that's true, can you and I possibly imagine the wonderful
things God has in store for us then? His promise is that it will be
bigger then, better then, more challenging and wonderful and
abundant and rewarding THEN. Even Everest will seem like nothing compared to the mountain peaks our Lord will lead us to scale
together with Him.

But your climb, and mine, can begin right now.

A Really High-Paying Temp Job

16
"IT'S FINE IF YOU OVERPAY *ME*"

The story is told of a man who went out into his driveway one day and found out that his beautiful new car had been stolen. What?! And he was really livid. How dare they? He hated being ripped off. Why couldn't the police control things? What was the matter with the mayor? And on and on. He was very frustrated, and rightly so, because he didn't deserve this.

Lo and behold, a little while later he went out again . . . and there was his car! Whoever had taken it had brought it back — and attached was a note. Apparently a man had run out of gas while rushing his wife to the delivery room at the hospital. Desperate, the husband had hotwired the nearest car and gotten his wife to the OB room just in time. And there on the dashboard, the "thief" had scotch-taped a big thank-you card, along with very expensive tickets to a sold-out play, coupons for dinner at a nice restaurant, etc.

Well! That was more like it! Now the man felt like the favors were rolling in his direction, and he felt much better. He didn't deserve this either, but bonuses and goodies were fine as long as he was the recipient.

So this man and his wife went to the restaurant and then out to the play, rejoicing all the while that they were getting such a marvelous deal, essentially for free. What good fortune! But you know, it wasn't actually that fortunate after all, because when the couple got back home they found a house that had been stripped completely bare of every single thing they owned. Furniture, money, jewels, silverware, everything. And of course, it was the same thief who had taken the car; the whole thing was a set-up, a scam designed to get this fellow out of his house for the evening. And our friend with the bare floors and the empty cupboards felt ripped off again.

One of the great truths of human experience is that we hate to be taken advantage of. The converse is also true; to be on the good end of a bargain is absolutely fine. Don't our eyes light up when the very thing we want in life is suddenly marked down to half price? In fact, sometimes we don't mind if it's marked wrong. We know it's a mistake on the part of the store, but if they want to put a $50 sticker on a $500 television set, we're the first in line.

As we continue through some of the very colorful parables that Jesus told, this one is probably the most baffling. It really is. I've entitled it: *A Really High-Paying Temp Job*, but most headings in the Bible say very simply: "The Parable of the Workers in the Vineyard." You'll find it in Matthew 20, and sometimes when you're studying something in chapter 20, it's not a bad idea to drift back to chapter 19 and find out what has led into this parable.

Right before this story about the really great temp job, a rich young man has just turned away in sorrow because the Savior had basically told him that if he wanted to get into heaven, he needed to liquidate his holdings, sell everything he had, give it all to the poor, and become a disciple. Well, the man wouldn't do it, couldn't do it. And even the disciples stood around saying, "Man, it's hard to be saved, I guess. Does anybody have a chance?"

And our friend Peter, always one with the math-oriented questions, has this one for Jesus: "We have left everything to follow You! What then will there be for us?"

And that's a fair question. Peter and eleven other men had really given up everything: family, friends, fishing boats, job security. Just to tramp around in dusty Judea with this itinerant Preacher who didn't have two shekels to rub together. So, of course, when Jesus says how very hard it is to qualify for heaven, Peter has to ask: "Well, are WE going to get any reward? We've been with You a long while here; where's the payoff?" And then Jesus tells this story.

"For the kingdom of heaven is like a landowner who went out early in the morning to hire men to work in his vineyard. He agreed to pay them a denarius for the day and sent them into his vineyard." It's a bit sobering that many of Jesus' stories begin with the line: "The kingdom of heaven is like" . . . such and such. Some of the stories contain what I've been calling "upside-down math." All the wrong people win in the end; they don't have politically correct Hollywood finishes hardly ever. And yet we have this clear teaching: "The kingdom of heaven follows the concepts of this story. What happens here in this vineyard is what's going to happen in the Church. The morals of this story are also the morals of the kingdom." It certainly makes the stories worth reading; that's for sure. But it's sometimes disquieting that such revolutionary ideology is going to be how things are when God takes over. So let's take a look.

Here are men who have agreed to work for the landowner. That's God, of course. These berry-pickers get a denarius for the day, which was the fair wage of that era. A decent paycheck for a long, hot 12-hour day in the sun.

Along around nine o'clock, "the third hour," as Jesus tells the story, the landowner goes to the marketplace and hires some more men. Only this time he signs them up this way: "You also go and work in my vineyard, and I will pay you whatever is right."

Notice, he doesn't specify this time what the pay will be. But he promises it will be fair. And I imagine the workers, in their minds, calculate down from one denarius for the whole day, and figure they'll get three-quarters of a denarius or whatever. Today the men would think: "The full-time guys were promised 75 bucks, so we'll get 55. Or maybe 52 or 57. But this boss looks okay; he said he'd be fair. We'll trust him."

Okay, the plot thickens. Around noon the boss man hires more men. "Go work and I'll pay you a fair wage for the rest of today."

Three o'clock, he signs up even more men. In fact, around five p.m., just an hour before quitting time, he goes back to the center of town where guys like this hang around swapping stories and sipping on diet Sprites, and he says: "Hey, why aren't you working?"

"'Cause nobody hired us," the men say.

"Well, I'll hire you. Quick, get out there to my vineyard. You can still get in an hour." And the men figure, "Well, five or six bucks is better than nothing. At least I can buy myself some supper." And they hustle out there and pick berries with the others until quitting time, which was at six o'clock.

As the gong sounds, the men line up to get their pay for the day. It's interesting that in Bible times — and this is a clear instruction from God in Leviticus 19 — people like this were supposed to be paid every single day at quitting time, for their own protection and financial welfare.

So what happens? The paymaster hands out cold cash, first of all, to the men who had just barely gotten there. They'd only been on the job for an hour. And what do you know? They get paid for a whole day! They score a full denarius, or today maybe the 75 bucks or whatever the going rate might be. But after working one hour — the coolest, breeziest hour of the day when things are already winding down — they're handed an envelope bulging with cash for twelve hours of work.

How do you suppose they responded? They could probably decide: "Man, this guy's a nut. He can't do math." But if they say that, they say it very quietly. They don't try hard to correct him. Or they think: "He's the best boss in the world. Wow! What generosity! This is 12 times what I thought I would get." Or they might think that it's just a flat-out mistake. Someone's computer has gone haywire, and is spitting out erroneous paychecks. Again, if they think that, they only think it to themselves. None of these men bother to offer their programming skills to fix what is obviously a biblical boo-boo.

How about the next batch, the men who came in at 3:00 p.m.? They get the exact same pay: a denarius. Now, that's still a hugely terrific deal, a major-league bargain, but not quite as good a deal as the five o'clock guys. So these men are torn: do they rejoice or complain? Are they being ripped off or are they lucky?

The men hired at noon — one denarius. The men hired at nine in the morning — one denarius. And here's the killer: the men who worked the whole steaming day, who put in the full 12 hours, who sweat through their clothes and only got a half-hour for lunch and got briars and thorns under all their fingernails . . . they get exactly one denarius. The same pay as the men who barely showed up at supper time. As Jesus tells the story, the master pays every man on the plantation the exact same amount.

And all of a sudden, this is a mess . . . the kind of mess God's kingdom is built on. Here's a very blunt question: is God . . . dare I say it? Is He a nut? Or as theologian F. W. Beare has dubbed our heavenly Father: "The Eccentric Employer"?

17
GETTING PAST ST. PETER AT THE GATE

In his colorful book, *Living Faith*, former U.S. President Jimmy Carter shares one of the types of anecdotes that people everywhere seem to love — of the genre where St. Peter is guarding the gate to heaven. Now, there's much that could be said about this particular brand of theology, but for the moment let's play along with our 39th president.

According to this particular bit of heavenly dialogue, a man comes up to the gate and wants to get in. Well, St. Peter does what he always seems to do in these exchanges. He says to the guy, "What are your credentials? Why do you deserve to enter here?" And the man hems and haws and shuffles his feet on the golden pavement because he can't think of much. But finally his face brightens. "Oh yes," he says. "During the Depression — I remember now — I saw a starving family on the street and I gave them 50 cents." And then he thinks and thinks and thinks some more, and finally something jogs his brain and he says, "Wait! There's more, I think. Not so long ago, my neighbor's house burned down, and I gave them an old table of mine that cost me half a buck." "Is that it?" Peter asks. "Yeah, I guess so."

Well, St. Peter has an angel check through the records and the computer files, and sure enough, the two reports are accurate. "What should I do?" the angel asks. And Peter, the guardian of the gate, gives a little shrug. "Aaah, give him his dollar back and tell him to go to hell."

Now, this little joke is from a chapter entitled "Reaching Out," where the president asks the very good question: "What good is our faith if it only expresses itself in a total of one dollar given away to needy and hurting people during a lifetime of selfish living?" And yet, as we read through a much less funny story found in Matthew 20, we have to post a large sign of warning around any joke or anecdote or story or sermon or book or *anything* which suggests that a man can arrive at the Pearly Gates of heaven and say, "I deserve to be here."

We're calling it the story of *A Really High-Paying Temp Job.* These days we might think of a person who's brought in as a sub to hack away at computer keys and rearrange web sites. And let's say he puts in a huge, frantic Wall Street kind of day — twelve hours. He's there staring at the screen until well after dark. But right close to quitting time, the owner of this hot little shop brings in a second computer nerd to work at the next terminal over. And he barely boots up his system and logs on before it's quitting time.

Lo and behold, when the company issues them each a check, the new kid gets paid for an entire day! Unbelievable! A full day's pay at temp agency rates, when he only worked an hour. And the technician who's been there since 6:30 a.m. feels his heart beat faster as he rips open his envelope. Because he ought to get about 12 times that much — if math proportions mean anything. But no . . . there on his check is the exact amount the agency had said he would get for the day: $113.79. And he notices that the one-hour worker has precisely that amount as well: $113.79. A one-hour worker and a twelve-hour worker make identical amounts.

So I'll ask as reverently as I can: is this Boss a nut? Is He crazy? There's no way this is fair! It may be legal — barely. It may not violate OSHA and the Division of Labor Standards Enforcement requirements — technically. After all, He did pay the first man the promised amount. But when you throw away huge sums on the second worker, the one who had it the easiest, that makes for tremendous turmoil in the workplace. This CEO is really steering His ship down the drain, isn't He?

Well, I say again, we pose these questions carefully and reverently. Because it's very clear that the landowner or the boss in this story is God Himself. And in the vineyard of Christian service, it's equally clear that the payscales are completely mixed up, messed up, upside-down and in total chaos. What kind of a Boss is this? And how should those on the short end of the stick — or the long end, too, for that matter — respond?

It's been pointed out that most of us identify with and immediately resonate with the person who worked all day. And as we read this Bible parable in Matthew 20, we're instantly mad. The boss says he'll pay you $113.79, and He does. So that should be fine. You work; you're paid. You're paid what it was promised you'd be paid. Everything is just really wonderful until you see that some-one else got as much as you for way less work. And instantly we are mad. Instantly! Why is that?

Well, one word, one human, world-centered word, tells us why. And that word is this: DESERVED. A person *deserved* a certain paycheck, and got way more. He got more than he *deserved*, and the rest of the workforce was instantly angry about it. You don't mind, maybe, getting what you don't deserve, but you sure don't want anyone else getting what they don't deserve.

Think about the story of Jonah, which kind of parallels this one. God told this wayward prophet to travel to Ninevah and scold the people, to warn them that destruction was imminent. They deserved to be wiped out. They were sinful, naughty, wicked peo-ple, and they all deserved to die. That was the message, and after swimming with a big fish for about three days, Jonah actually went to Ninevah and told the people what they deserved.

Only problem is: God ends up forgiving the whole city. He "changes His mind." Instead of paying the people zero — or pay-ing them the hot flames they deserve — God gives them the huge paycheck of grace and forgiveness.

And how does Jonah react? He's boiling mad! "But Jonah was greatly displeased and became angry. He prayed to the Lord, 'O

Lord, is this not what I said when I was still at home? That is why I was so quick to flee to Tarshish. I knew that You are a gracious and compassionate God, slow to anger and abounding in love, a God who relents from sending calamity. Now, O Lord, take away my life, for it is better for me to die than to live."

I think I can guarantee you that the residents of Ninevah were a lot happier about God's forgiveness than Jonah was. But you see, he was God's 12-hour man! (Except for the very long lunch break he took, where he ran off in the opposite direction.) He was a prophet; he'd been faithful and obedient. He deserved God's favor, and these Ninevites didn't. And so when the payscale got tampered with, he was beside himself with frustration. "How can I trust You," he lamented to God, "if You're going to treat people with kindness and forgiveness? I worked so hard in Your vineyard, and You pay me back by making a fool of me."

Time and again, this same pattern is shown. A thief dying on the cross repents at the last possible moment. In his book, *What's So Amazing About Grace?*, Philip Yancey writes: "In one of His last acts before death, Jesus forgave a thief dangling on a cross, knowing full well the thief had converted out of plain fear. That thief would never study the Bible, never attend synagogue or church, and never make amends to all those he had wronged. He simply said 'Jesus, remember me,' and Jesus promised, 'Today you will be with Me in paradise.' It was another shocking reminder that grace does not depend on what we have done for God but rather what God has done for us."

And here's OSHA complaint #3. The new Christian church was beside itself with frustration over the fact that Gentiles were going to be allowed to slip in the back door. How could this be? They weren't the chosen people! They hadn't followed Jehovah in the wilderness for 40 years. Why should they be so overpaid? And yet, as Jesus tells us this offbeat little vineyard story, this is the way of the kingdom of God.

Well, there's tons more where this came from, but I guess we should just return to St. Peter at the gate. If you or I ever once think that we can approach God and God's kingdom with the thought that we *deserve* something, that concept has got to go. It's got to be destroyed or, better yet, crucified.

Have you given away lots of money? Have you done a lot of good deeds? Especially in contrast to your neighbor down the street? Does that then mean that you deserve heaven, or at least a little bit more of heaven than the next guy? That thought has got to go. The word "deserve" has got to go. The word "paycheck" has got to go. The word "earn" has got to go.

Robert Farrar Capon once wrote: "If the world could have been saved by good bookkeeping, it would have been saved by Moses, not Jesus."

And as Philip Yancey discusses this very vineyard story, he hits the nail right on the head. Listen: "Grace cannot be reduced to generally accepted accounting principles. In the bottom-line realm of ungrace, some workers deserve more than others; in the realm of grace the word *deserve* does not even apply."

18
SOMEBODY GIVE POOR BILL GATES A DOLLAR

There was a frustrating little *Reader's Digest* story out not too long ago about our prospering friend, Mr. Bill Gates. I don't know what his personal net worth is now, but according to these calculations, if he were to buy a $250,000 sports car — like a Lambourghini — it would be like you or me spending 67 cents. That's how much it would hurt. Sixty-seven cents. This same little math vignette suggested that if Mr. Gates were to see a hundred-dollar bill lying on the sidewalk, it literally would not be worth the two seconds it would take to bend over and pick it up. It'd be like straining your back to pick up a penny — or in old England, a ha'penny. You just wouldn't bother.

What's that got to do with this Bible parable where a very intense emphasis is placed on money and who's got how much? We've already suggested that it's dangerous, maybe even fatal, to have the word "deserve" in the Christian vocabulary. "*I deserve* such-and-such pay." "*I deserve* a mansion in heaven." "*I deserve* a high position in God's government, a seat right next to Jesus at the Last Supper." As a person stands in the shadow of the cross of Calvary, it's foolish to think that we deserve any kind of paycheck at all at the end of the day.

Here's Philip Yancey's take on this parable, as quoted in his book, *What's So Amazing About Grace?* "We risk missing the story's point: that God dispenses gifts, not wages. None of us gets paid according to merit, for none of us comes close to satisfying God's requirements for a perfect life. If paid on the basis of fairness, we would all end up in hell."

Our theme verse here at the Voice of Prophecy screams it through a megaphone: "For it is by grace you have been saved, through faith — and this not from yourselves, it is the gift of God — not by works, so that no one can boast." (Ephesians 2:8,9)

So in one sense, at least, if the words "deserve" and "earn" and "paycheck" come out of our vocabularies, then what is the point of this story?

One thing we can learn for sure is that Jesus is telling us this: don't keep your eyes on your fellow workers. Don't look at what others are paid. Don't pay a lot of attention to how Bill Gates is being treated. Just focus on your own relationship with Me. Because one thing is true in this story: not one person was underpaid. No none was cheated. The owner did live up to every bargain; He fulfilled all promises. And people only got into trouble and into a murmuring spirit when they began to look around at the pay stubs of their peers.

There's a quiet little story right at the end of the gospels where none less than Jesus Himself tells someone to just plain mind their own business. Christ has just had a bit of a loving confrontation with Peter, who had denied Him before the crucifixion. And here in John 21, He very kindly tells His restored disciple Peter that one day he's going to die a martyr's death, just like Jesus. Which is all right with Peter. He accepts that tough news. But just a moment later he looks around and sees John standing nearby. And, maybe instinctively, he asks Jesus: "What will happen to him?"

And Jesus tells him this: "If I want him to remain alive until I return, what is that to you? You must follow Me."

In other words, that wasn't something Peter needed to know. How God was going to treat John wasn't a concern for Peter. The bottom line for Peter was that Christ was going to sustain him, see him through, empower his ministry, be with him when he picked up his own cross, and finally guarantee him a home in heaven. That was the package for Peter, and that's all Peter needed to know.

There was a lot of huffing and puffing here in Los Angeles at the start of the 1998 season about the salaries of baseball players. And in response to that, the L.A. Times printed out the annual pay package for every player on all 30 major league clubs who was getting more than a million dollars a year. Which is just about everyone, it seems. But it's interesting that on any one team, there will be a Mr. Big, a superstar, who's getting eight or nine or ten million. Then a couple who get five, one or two who get maybe 2.3 million, and then several players who just get a million. Maybe the batboy gets a million. Well, I'm kidding, but there are also players on that same team who only get maybe $200,000. And they're on the same team, playing on the same field, as a guy who is getting ten million for playing the same game. And especially on a night where the superstar trillionaire makes two errors and strikes out five times, there could be some rumbling in the clubhouse afterwards. "Why is this man making so much more than I am? This is unfair! I want to renegotiate my salary!"

 I'm embarrassed to even look through it now, but way back in the very first book I scratched my way through writing, *Bats, Balls & Altar Calls*, I discussed this very parable about the salaries and the hurt feelings, and then applied them to a ball team which goes on to win the World Series. And here's a point for Christians to consider: "The fact is, the harvest came in. The overriding goal was reached. The championship was won. And if some workers made more than others, or had better batting averages, so what? 'Don't worry so much about what's happening in the lives of others,' Jesus says. 'You keep your bargain with Me, and things will be all right for you. You may make a little more or a little less than others in this life. Perhaps you'll be famous; perhaps not. But if you labor in My vineyard, eternal life will be yours."

And we have as an example the experience of Peter. How long did this wild and woolly disciple serve Jesus? His whole adult life — with beatings and trials and nights in jail and persecutions and then a crucifixion at the end. How long did the thief on the cross serve Jesus? A few minutes, maybe an hour or so. What reward did they both receive? An eternal life in God's kingdom, living in mansions with the identical floor plans. Is that okay with the thief? Sure. Is it okay with Peter? I'm sure he'll be happy with that arrangement as well.

Here's the bottom line. Whether you live in relationship with Jesus Christ and serve Him for one day or for 95 years in the mission field, the reward is the same. You will get an eternity — not a hundred years, not a thousand, not a million, billion, or trillion — but an eternity of a life greater and richer and more abundant than you can imagine. We'd never try to describe it for our listeners on the radio because we'd be idiots if we thought we could do it. But you and I and that thief on the cross and the mass murderer on Death Row who has a deathbed conversion, are all going to get that same paycheck. We're all going to get mansions. And we're going to live in them for a very, very, very long time.

With that in mind, does the concept of a little bit more pay, or a little bit less pay, or a slight discrepancy in the scale down here, for these few years on this little planet, really matter? No! It doesn't matter! This isn't the real game down here! Down here, this is nothing! And Jesus tells us this parable to remind us to keep our eyes on the real prize. If we get hung up comparing things down here, figuring out who deserved what — when that word *deserved* shouldn't even be in the lexicon — then we've missed the boat.

For the mathematicians among us, we could well think of that sideways-eight which indicates "infinity." And when your prize is "infinity" you can't get more than that. You can't add to infinity. It would be like you giving Bill Gates a dollar. Or him getting upset if you *didn't* give him a dollar. People who have as many billions as he does in the bank really do not worry about the dollar, or about the paycheck for one hour or even one long day in the vineyard. Their eyes are on bigger prizes than that.

19
SO MAD AT AMADEUS

There was a fascinating story here in the local paper a week or so ago (Spring '98) about the very thriving business of being a political consultant. These are the media pros who simply know how to run campaigns. And if you sign them up, they can make your TV ads, help coordinate your schedule, do what's called "oppo" work on the enemy candidates, tell you what to say and think, design position papers, and all the rest.

Of course, many of these people are available to just about any candidate from the right, the left, the middle, Democrat, Republican, or Green Party. Especially any Green Party candidate who's got green money. That's the bottom line, of course. And we think immediately of people like the infamous Dick Morris, who used to work just with conservative Republicans, it seemed, but all of a sudden was brought in — for a price — to save the Clinton presidency.

The dilemma happening more and more, these days, is that of switching horses halfway through. A candidate will hire a consultant and, of course, he or she's got to pretty much put their life into the handler's hands. They've got to confide secrets, reveal closet skeletons, bare their soul. And more than once, now, for whatever reason, a political consultant will jump ship and go over to the opposite camp where the grass is greener and the money too. And this has provoked a thorny question of ethics: once this handler is armed with secrets from one side, is he or she free to share that dirt with the opposition, with the new boss?

Well, it's a lively discussion, but let's consider the concept of commitment instead. There comes a time in a person's life when they've got to simply pick a boss and stay with him. In a way, these consultants are like surfers in the Pacific Ocean who float on their surfboards, wearing their wet suits and waiting for the right wave. And when it looks like it's coming along, they paddle for all they're worth and hope to ride that winning wave all the way to the shore of victory. Any consultant who endlessly jumps around, going for a few more bucks here, a higher title there, betraying confidences right and left, is only going to experience limited short-term success.

Here in Matthew 20, it may appear to tell about a boss who doesn't seem too bright. At the end of the day, he pays people what he promised, but in a very strange way. Those who worked the least amount of time get the same pay as those who have been on the campaign from the beginning. A campaign worker who didn't sign on until November 1, just two days before the election, gets the same pay as a George Stephanopoulos who's been on duty seven days a week for the last six months. Or the aide who's served the boss since he was a lowly governor down in Arkansas.

And so the question is very important here: is this a Boss you can trust? If the pay scales seem all messed up, and if certain people — never you, for some reason — get paid more than they deserve, should you stay with this Leader? Or should you ride some other wave?

In the Bible parable itself, the first workers are told very plainly how much they'll be paid. "One denarius, a standard day's pay, for a day's work." But workers who come along later hear this plantation owner tell them: "Please come work for Me, and I'll pay you what's fair." Well, who's to know how much that will be? But these workers trust Him, and things work out very, very well for every single one of them. They're all paid way more than any of them expected or deserved.

Of course, where the story bogs down — in human terms — is when the Owner pays OTHER people too much money. The all-day workers don't think He's mistreated them; they just resent how the Boss has overpaid all the other campaign staffers. And of course, this is where just about all of us reveal by our whining that we plain and simple do not understand or comprehend or accept what Calvary and grace are all about.

In *What's So Amazing About Grace?*, Philip Yancey describes how he went to the play, *Amadeus*, which was also the Oscar-winning Best Picture back in the year 1984.

"[This] play . . . shows a composer in the seventeenth century," he writes, "seeking to understand the mind of God. The devout Antonio Salieri has the earnest desire, but not the aptitude, to create immortal music of praise. It infuriates him that God has instead lavished the greatest gift of musical genius ever known on an impish preadolescent named Wolfgang Amadeus Mozart."

And all through the story, this aching anger and jealousy just eat at the older man. Why, oh why, oh why? God, what is the matter with You? This . . . this . . . kid, this profane, foul-mouthed, promiscuous child whose high-pitched giggling laugh desecrates the halls of the great cathedrals and palaces of Europe, is just brimming over with God-given talent. It's so insufferably easy for Mozart! And Salieri, who is a humble and obedient and loyal servant, both to God and king, simply can't compete. He can't compose as well, play as well, create as effectively. It's just not there. It's a case of getting a smaller paycheck from heaven, and no matter how much he cries or howls or schemes, God doesn't fix the situation.

It appears that the heavenly Father is truly a bad Boss. In an irony of ironies, as Yancey points out, the very name "Amadeus" actually means "beloved of God." Why in the world does God love this profane, powder-wigged prodigy?

And in your life and mine, we can see the same ripoff being played over and over a million times. Someone else out there is always doing better than us. God is blessing them more, treating them better, giving them more favors. We'd like to be able to preach or sing or write great Broadway plays, but no matter how tightly we grip that pencil or practice our oratory, it's just not there. God, the mysterious vineyard Owner, has messed up the payscale again.

And Yancey runs down a little list from right in the Bible, because this just happens over and over: "Why would God choose Jacob the conniver over dutiful Esau? Why confer supernatural powers of strength on a Mozartian delinquent named Samson? Why groom a runty shepherd boy, David, to be Israel's king? And why bestow a sublime gift of wisdom on Solomon, the fruit of that king's adulterous liaison? Indeed, in each of these Old Testament stories the scandal of grace rumbles under the surface until finally, in Jesus' parables, it bursts forth in a dramatic upheaval to reshape the moral landscape."

So this is heaven's way. Once again, the math of the kingdom of heaven is just plain upside-down. Two and two is never four; it's five, and then ten, and a hundred and a thousand . . . especially when God is paying *other* people. For you, two and two is four, but not for all the jerky Amadeuses all around you. And this is fixed; this is how it is.

In his Matthew commentary for the Tyndale series, Richard France reasserts that this is the unavoidable nature of heaven, folks: "The essential point of the parable is that God is like that; His generosity transcends human ideas of fairness. No one receives less than they deserve, but some receive far more."

He then goes on to hit us — Antonio Salieri and you and me — right where it hurts. Right between the eyes. Notice and wince along with me: "God's grace to the undeserving," he writes, "should be a cause for joy, not for jealousy."

And you say, "I'm not ready for that." Well, maybe none of us are. It sticks in the throat when God blesses someone else, when the worst person you know gets a favor from heaven. When it looks like the #1 scoundrel of your city is going to be saved in heaven and have a mansion as big as yours. And at that point, as we feel our blood boiling, we have to stop and ask ourselves: "What has God done for me? Hasn't He saved me too? Am I not going to receive a full eternity in His kingdom? Don't I have the same abundant, overly generous paycheck as the others . . . in terms of the forever of His eternal government in heaven? Didn't God expend the full treasury, the bottomless well of Calvary's grace, for me just as He did for my neighbor?" And then, as we stand in the shadow of the Cross, maybe we'll quiet down a bit and praise God for being the kind of Boss He is.

Theologian R. H. Stein, in his book, *An Introduction to the Parables of Jesus*, makes this very probing point. "It is frightening to realize that our identification with the first workers, and hence with the opponents of Jesus, reveals how loveless and unmerciful we basically are. We may be more 'under law' in our thinking and less 'under grace' than we realize. God is good and compassionate far beyond His children's understanding!"

Does that diagnosis hit home? Are we mad when God favors others? If so, is it possible that we haven't yet experienced grace? Back to Dr. Richard France, who makes this gentle suggestion in his *Matthew* commentary: "Parables are characteristically open-ended, and a general rule for their interpretation is, 'If the cap fits, wear it!'"

Hmmmmm. I'm afraid mine fits rather snugly. How about yours?

20

POOR HARRY WORKED ALL DAY, AND FOR WHAT?

So many of the parables of Jesus feature nameless, anonymous people, but that's about to change! In this final look at this story of the workers in the vineyard, I'd like for you to meet one of the specific people in the lineup.

We're still in Matthew 20, of course, and there are many, many vineyard workers milling around at the paymaster's table. Now, some of them have put in a long, tiring twelve-hour day. They've got grape stains on their clothes, kinks in their backs, scrapes on their knees, and blisters on their fingers. Other men didn't start working until noon, others not until 3:00 p.m., and a lucky little group who only put in one hour. And the reason I say "lucky" is because, as things turn out in Jesus' story, every single man in the work force gets the exact same pay. To the penny! Now, it's a very fair wage for an entire day of work; nobody can complain there. Except that the half-day boys and even the fellows who only put in a single hour of work — sixty cool and breezy minutes at the very end — get that same amount. In the Bible, a denarius. Today it'd be 60 or 70 or 80 bucks.

Now in the Bible story, the men who had worked all day and then got that same 80 bucks or whatever, immediately began to complain. "This is unfair!" they hollered. "What's the matter with this boss?" And so on.

But right here I'd like for you to meet one of the workers who did indeed work that entire 12-hour-day, that long hot shift in the sun, and didn't say a single word of complaint.

Our vineyard worker is Harry. That's his real name, actually. Dr. Harry Miller. As soon as I say that, many of you recognize him: the famous "China Doctor." For many, many decades this genius of medicine worked for God in the exotic but steaming hot, crowded cities of faraway China. I mean, he went out there in the year 1903 with his young bride, Maude. Groaning their way over the Pacific Ocean in a tiny stateroom just over the propeller shaft of the ill-named freighter, the *Empress of India*, it was hardly a royal ride! By the time they got to China, Harry had been seasick for so long he vowed to just live in the Orient for the rest of his life and never return to the United States.

Well, I could take 200 pages and simply purloin huge sections of the wonderful book, *China Doctor*, by Raymond S. Moore. But this brilliant surgeon literally gave his life to the country of China. He spent decades there, but just two years after arriving, he buried his wife, who died of a mysterious foreign ailment at the age of 25. He started many Christian hospitals; he survived the wars and rebellions. He lived as a Chinese person, even dressing in the Oriental robes and wearing his hair in the queue, or traditional pigtail. He operated on peasants and royalty alike.

In fact, he was finally awarded the coveted Blue Star of China, by none other than Generalissimo Chiang Kai-shek and Madame Chiang Kai-shek, for all of his spiritual and humanitarian work in their country.

But there's quite a bit more to this story of a quiet and faithful worker in the vineyard. Because Harry Miller, as renowned as he was, also served some brief stints in the U.S. where his inventive surgical procedures made him famous. He served as an attending physician to presidents Taft and Wilson. He treated William Jennings Bryan and Alexander Graham Bell. Many, many fabulously wealthy celebrities sought him out. But in all that time, did he become wealthy? Did he increase his paycheck?

A hospital worker recalled once how a famous Florida millionaire came to the Washington Adventist Sanitarium, desperate to be cured. Top specialists hadn't been able to spot his troubles, but Miller quickly diagnosed the problem and cured him. Grateful beyond words, the man paid his hospital bill and then asked to see the China Doctor. Expressing his thanks almost with tears coming down his cheeks, this recovered millionaire took out a brand new, clean, starch-stiff thousand dollar bill — the first any of the employees had ever seen — and pressed it into Dr. Miller's hand. This was his personal gift of appreciation. And this was back in the 1920s. Dr. Miller, at that time, was receiving a salary of exactly $44 a week.

But just moments later, the humble doctor turned and gave the bill to his assistant. "Here, Stan," he said. "Take this down to the cashier." During his entire career, in China and the U.S. both — and he often received huge gifts from Chinese royalty and wealthy patrons — friends estimate that he turned over to the mission work personal gifts totaling at least $2.5 million. One wealthy ruler, the infamous "Young Marshal," who kicked an opium addiction under Miller's supervision, handed him a personal check for $50,000. The China Doctor endorsed it immediately into a trust fund to build a Seventh-day Adventist hospital in Lanchow. Over in China, while many doctors drove around in luxurious U.S. automobiles, or even had chauffeur-driven limousines, Dr. Miller could be seen rumbling through the narrow streets of Shanghai in an old, beat-up Dodge convertible that had the top missing.

Well, I could go on and on because the anecdotes on this man just don't end. I don't have the exact dates, but I think that Dr. Miller lived to be something like 93 or 94, and was still in service to his God right to the very end. Even in his 80s he was traveling around the world, still starting hospitals, still witnessing for the Lord through his exceptional talents.

Well, what's the upshot of this kind of story? Here's a man who worked in the vineyard for the Owner for the full shift. In fact, this was no 12-hour day; it was 15 or 16. He gave a long, long lifetime of hot, sweating, standing-in-lines-for-Communist-interrogation service for his God. And at the end of the day, the paycheck was not very spectacular. This man who could have been a multi-multi-millionaire died and was buried in a very modest grave, without much of an estate to leave behind.

So I ask the question one final time: what's the reward? These workers in the vineyard all received a denarius, a penny, at the end of the day. And the moral has certainly been that there's a larger reward called eternal life. There's heaven and golden streets and a beautiful River of Life and a land that's fairer than day. And the China Doctor was a man who knew he was going there. He knew there was a place being prepared for him, a place where he would see again the bride of his youth, young Maude Miller. He knew he would live and dwell with Jesus for all of eternity. So is that the reward?

Just a few verses earlier, before Jesus began to tell this story, He gave Peter an answer when this disciple asked Him, shekel-signs gleaming in his eyes: "What's our reward for having followed You so faithfully?" And Jesus told him: "Anyone who follows Me and leaves houses and lands and family and friends for My sake will receive a hundred times as much . . . AND inherit eternal life." So is this the payoff? Is this what makes the story of the vineyard turn out all right?

Well, yes, it is. But I'd like to suggest something more. And if you've ever looked on with frustration at those who live a life of flowing money and debauchery and cocaine parties, and then just jumped on the Jesus Train at the last possible minute — just in time to get the same full paycheck as you — I'd like for us to think of the perspective of the China Doctor. He's sleeping in Jesus now, but what if you were to ask him: "Do you feel cheated? You could have been wealthy. You could have had so much. But you worked in China for God all those years"? How would he respond?

Pastor Morris Venden answers on behalf of Dr. Harry Miller in his book, *Parables of the Kingdom.* He asks: "So what is the reward? What is the penny, [the denarius]? It is Jesus Himself! He can't give the twelve-hour workers more than the one-hour workers, because He can give neither more nor less than Himself. Why? Because in giving Himself He gives all the riches of the universe."

Let me put it this way. Which workers got to spend the whole day with Jesus? It was those who were there 12 hours. Which ones got the most fellowship? The ones who were there 12 hours. Which ones experienced the adventure of serving side by side with the most wonderful Savior? The ones who worked 12 hours. If you wanted just money, yes, maybe they were ripped off. But if you wanted Jesus, and closeness with Jesus, and fellowship with Jesus, and partnership with Jesus, then who were the luckiest guys in the world? The ones who worked 12 hours.

In her book, *Steps to Christ*, author E. G. White takes the same view: "God might have committed the message of the gospel, and all the work of loving ministry, to the heavenly angels." He doesn't really NEED Dr. Miller, or you, or me. She continues: "He might have employed other means for accomplishing His purpose. But in His infinite love He chose to make us co-workers with Himself, with Christ and the angels, that we might share the blessing, the joy, the spiritual uplifting, which results from this unselfish ministry."

Are there frustrations out there in the vineyard? Is it hot? Sometimes messy? Almost always fatiguing? Yes to all of the above. But that's where Jesus is. And you know — there's no place I'd rather work.

The Good Guy From the Bad Neighborhood

21

THE HERO AT 7-ELEVEN

Frank was a senior citizen, a widower who'd lost his wife, Estelle, nearly three years ago. Fixed income, retired, with Social Security and a very small pension. He had a little house, which had been in a not-too-bad neighborhood in the early 70s, but by now it had fallen into what people used to call "the wrong side of the railroad tracks." Gangs had moved in; crack had taken over. Street hookers were more and more open about their business. Police didn't come by very often, and when they did it was a pretty cursory visit. In and out quick.

Frank really would have liked to move out and into a better neighborhood, or maybe even down to Florida. Because frankly, he didn't like the people who lived on his block anymore. They were noisy, they were careless and unemployed; they were a vastly different skin shade than he was. Everything they did seemed to kind of feed the various stereotypes he'd always carried around anyway.

But like it or not, this was going to be his neighborhood until he died, because he couldn't afford better. In fact, he didn't even have a car anymore; unless he pooled with someone, he couldn't even get to a grocery store in an upscale area. So he bought all of his necessities like milk and razor blades at the corner 7-Eleven. And sometimes his guts tightened as he passed by the tough kids who hung out there with their skateboards and their black tank tops and their bandannas and their muttered obscenities. He never said anything to them, but his mind was always racing with the things he'd like to say. It was always a relief to unlock his own front door, undo the second deadbolt, plop his little bag of groceries on the scarred Formica table, and lock things back up tight.

And then one day, the thing he'd always feared might happen . . . actually did. He was out of bread and cooking oil, and Gary, his once-in-a-while car-loaning friend, was away to take care of his sister. So Frank, taking just the few dollars he knew he'd need, walked slowly to the 7-Eleven again, noticing the new batch of ugly graffiti, most of it unintelligible. "Stupid punks," he muttered to himself. "They write stuff . . . and nobody knows what it means." Then he realized that it was probably better that way, but it still made him boil inside. He was about half a block from the crowded parking lot of the convenience store when a huge black car came by real slow, with the back end jacked up about a foot-and-a-half, and with all of its subwoofers blaring out rap music that went right through pedestrians.

And then a shot rang out.

For just a second, the kids in the parking lot thought the car had backfired. And then they saw Frank, this aging, lonely, angry, beaten-up man crumpled next to the curb, blood oozing from a wound in his shoulder.

And everybody just froze. For about five seconds they just stood there. The car was moving away from the store, and they watched as it picked up speed and kept going down the street. No motive, no message. Just a random act of violence, a drive-by shooting. That was all it was. And the kids and the customers just stood there.

A couple of the teenagers went over about halfway and got a closer look. "Man, he's bleeding bad," one of them said. But they didn't know if it was dangerous to touch him, or if the car might be coming back, or just what to do. So they kind of moved back, walking backwards, until they were in the parking lot again. "Anybody call the cops?" a woman asked. "I think the guy in the store will," a nine-year-old boy said. "He usually does." He said it like — "Well, that's his job. This happens all the time around here, lady."

On the other side of the street, filling up his tank at the Arco self-serve station, was a preacher. He'd pulled off the freeway because he was down to fumes. And he, too, heard the one shot ring out. He saw the senior citizen jerk once, then fall down on the pavement. And about fifteen seconds later, the gas pump clicked off, and the Man of God stood there, transfixed.

"What do I do?" He was supposed to meet a wealthy donor at a restaurant in 40 minutes. This was a man who'd hinted he was about ready to contribute $25,000 to the church building program. And he didn't like to be kept waiting.

For just a moment, the preacher, out of habit, almost started to cross the street. Then he saw the gang members down at the 7-Eleven. He saw the blood oozing onto Frank's gray flannel shirt. He pictured in his mind the mess, the hot tar of the pavement getting on his pants, the blood on his hands, the smell of sweat and the odors of this rough ghetto neighborhood on his clothes. And very slowly, feeling a twinge, but only a twinge, a quick-passing twinge of guilt, he put the nozzle back, twisted the gas cap into place, and pulled back onto the freeway. "Somebody will call 911," he said to himself. "That's not my job; it's their job." And he was less than a mile down the interstate before he'd completely forgotten it.

Another man heard the same gunshot, and kind of froze up morally too. He was a deacon of a church about eight blocks away, but he always came over here during his lunch break because there was a funky little used book store that sometimes had the great religious classics for a quarter or fifty cents. In fact, this very afternoon he'd scored a dog-eared copy of *Peace With God*, Billy Graham's very first book — an autographed copy! For just two bucks! And as he came out of the bookstore and stepped into the hot sunshine, he heard the muffled little *pop*! and saw Frank collapse.

And again there was that moment of wrestling. "Is this my problem? I'm just a visiting shopper here, out of my usual suburban cocoon." He watched the teenagers in their own slow-motion reaction — some kids moving hesitantly toward the fallen man, others going into the store, others easing away. One boy, holding his skateboard, was over at the payphone; was he calling for an ambulance? The deacon couldn't tell.

But he glanced at his watch and noticed with a bit of relief that he was late. There was no way he could stop and check. He'd be late getting back to Century 21, where he was the top salesman. And he had escrow papers from three big deals sitting there on his desk. One of them was a sale to a Hollywood couple, and he hoped he might even have a chance to say something to them about God the next time they got together to work on the financing. He better get back to that, and trust that someone here, someone who belonged here and knew the ways and the rhythms of this neighborhood, would take care of things. So very quickly, glancing around to see if that ominous black car might be circling back, he punched in the numbers for his new keyless-entry leased car, and drove away without looking back.

And Frank lay there on the pavement. Five minutes went by. Six. Seven. He was still conscious, but feeling weaker by the second. The blood wasn't flowing quickly, but he could tell that it was still seeping through his shirt. It was all over his face, and the little granules of sand and concrete particles were pressing into the scarlet streaks on his cheek. "Somebody help me," he tried to say, but his voice was drowned out by the traffic. "Please. Somebody."

And then he heard a voice. "Hey, man. You okay?"

He couldn't turn his head even, but he could barely make out the form of a teenager. One of the kids at the 7-Eleven. Blue jeans, a ratty white shirt with nothing but the picture of a fist on it. The boy had put down his skateboard and was kneeling next to him. "Man, you're hit bad," the boy said, his words softened by his accent. "Those guys nailed you in the shoulder, looks like."

"Please . . . don't hurt me." Frank felt his weakened pulse fluttering for a moment. Would this street punk finish him off, take the three dollars he had in his pocket? "Can you . . . call 911 for me?"

"I already did, man." The boy took off his bandanna and began to gently dab at the blood on Frank's face. "But they're slow. Really slow. 'Specially around here. By the time they get to us, you'll die for sure. Or at least melt in this sun."

And all at once, Frank, this senior citizen with a bullet in his shoulder, found himself in the back seat of a classic Ford Mustang. And this skateboarding boy from the 'hood, and his fellow gang member, were driving their human cargo a mile and a half to the emergency room of the county hospital. Helping the orderly get Frank onto a stretcher. Waiting for an hour and fifteen minutes while doctors took a look at him. And — wonder of wonders — when the clerk at E.R. said that they had to have a signature, or a Medicare card, or an insurance number, or *some* kind of co-pay before they could do anything at all, this kid from 7-Eleven dug into the pocket of his jeans, and pulled out a twenty-dollar bill. "That's what I get pouring concrete every weekend," he told the clerk. "Take it. And if you need more, I can get it . . . but probably not till Sunday."

"Can't your friend pay?" the nursing clerk asked him, her voice suddenly soft with a bit of awe, like she was experiencing something right out of the Bible.

"My friend?" The kid laughed, his amusement bouncing off the block walls of the un-airconditioned waiting room. "Are you kidding? Man, I never saw that guy before in my life."

22

AFRAID TO EVEN SAY THE "S" WORD

"And who IS my neighbor?"

That little five-word question came from a man who plied Jesus with one in a seemingly endless flow of trick questions. But Christ had an answer for him, a story, a parable, which has resonated ever since, right down here to today. "Who is my neighbor? Who am I really supposed to love?"

They say the world loves a story, but Hollywood's back alleys are filled with scripts that got rejected, sitcoms that got canceled, and film stories that went into turnaround and never got made. And the reason some stories don't work is because they don't apply to how people live! Well, if there was ever a parable from the Bible which still works — big-time — nearly 2000 years after it was first told, this has got to be that story. The parable of the Good Samaritan, which answers the question: "Who is my neighbor?"

There are two stories in the book of Luke where a man asks Jesus Christ: "What do I have to do to inherit eternal life?" Here in chapter 10, and another similar anecdote in chapter 18. In that passage, Jesus says to the man, "Well, keep all of the command-ments." "Oh, I already do that," the ruler replies with a confident smile. "Ever since I was a boy. Is there anything else?" "Yes," Jesus tells him, "Sell everything you have, give the money to the poor, and then come follow Me. Be My disciple." And the man goes away sad, because he's a millionaire.

Now here in chapter 10, Jesus gives quite a different answer to what's essentially the same question. Consider this reply from Jesus, and decide for yourself if this response is easier or harder.

Actually, Christ knows that this man is trying to catch him in a verbal trap. The Bible says this "expert in the law" stood up to test

Jesus. In the King James: "And, behold, a certain lawyer stood up, and tempted Him."

Jesus sees the trap a mile off, of course, so he wisely lets the man answer his own question. I'm reminded of the Jewish rabbi who was asked by a frustrated student: "How come you teachers always answer questions with another question?" And the aging wise one responds: "So what's wrong with a question?" But Jesus says to the man: "What is written in the law? How do you read it?"

And the man gives this answer: "'Love the Lord your God with all your heart and with all your soul and with all your strength and with all your mind,' and, 'Love your neighbor as yourself.'"

And that was a good answer, quoting directly from Deuteronomy 6 and Leviticus 19. Jesus gives him an encouraging nod: "'You have answered correctly,' Jesus replied. 'Do this and you will live.'"

But think for a moment about the difficulty of this requirement. Maybe it seems soft to you — softer, anyway, than having a huge garage sale where you sell not only the things *in* your garage, but the garage itself . . . and the house and the whole thing, so that you can give everything to the poor.

But are you and I and this John Grisham lawyer really capable of loving God with all of our heart? And with all of our soul and our strength and our mind? One-hundred-and-ten percent commitment, all day every day? Is that something we can do? Are we coming close? And then to love our neighbor as our self? Because Jesus wasn't just handing out a Hallmark card here — "Love your neighbor and hug a tree." He was actually saying this, and meaning it. We have to love God with everything we've got, every fiber of emotion and heart and soul there is in us. And then we have to love our neighbor with that same intensity.

In his recent book, *Living Faith*, President Jimmy Carter describes how back in the 1960s he partnered up with a Cuban-American pastor named Eloy Cruz for a summer of witnessing. And this man had a passion for people: simple people, poor people, struggling people. He and Carter would sit in the kitchen of some home where the people had tremendous problems and challenges to face. And somehow Pastor Cruz knew just the words to share, the best way to explain his own love for them and for his Savior Jesus. Time after time, Jimmy Carter would see tears flow and people respond spiritually to that love. And this quiet, dynamic missionary pastor had a slogan that comes right out of this story. "Love God," he would say, "and the person in front of you."

And in our Bible story, as this sharpie lawyer tries to jockey with Jesus a bit, pin Him down with debating points, he's at a stalemate. Because he and Jesus agree on this answer. "Love God with all your heart; love your neighbor with all your heart." Not that this man was accomplishing those twin objectives, you understand. But he knew how to give the textbook answer, and Jesus had given him an A. So where should he go next?

Well, this lawyer takes the easy way out. He asks another question, one which feeds right into the popular discussion of that era. "All right, then, Mr. Jesus, tell me this," he asks. "Just who is my neighbor? Who do I have to be nice to? Who do I have to love?"

And you see, immediately there was a buzz of interest and approval. Because this was a point of constant, coffee-house debate in Israel. Who was your neighbor? Just the two families living on either side of you? Or everyone on your entire cul-de-sac?

There were a couple of "givens" in society back then. If you were talking about the heathen . . . well, that wasn't even on the table. Nonbelievers weren't your neighbors; they weren't anything. Even Jesus called them "dogs" — or seemed to — on one occasion at least. They were of absolutely no account, no worth, no anything. Nobody who'd graduated from kindergarten would even discuss that.

And how about Samaritans? Could they possibly qualify as "neighbors"? Not a chance! Not if they lived in your own back-yard, which wasn't about to happen. The New International Version text notes for the Bible give us this bit of illumination: "Jews viewed Samaritans as half-breeds, both physically and spiri-tually. . . . [Samaritans were] a mixed-blood race resulting from the intermarriage of: Israelites left behind when the people of the northern kingdom exiled, and Gentiles brought into the land by the Assyrians."

Speaking of spiritually, the Samaritans only accepted the Pentateuch as their Bible, rejecting all of the other writings held so dear by the Jews. There was a debate, where the Samaritans had their temple on the "wrong" mountain, Gerazim, instead of on Zion, which was, of course, the right and proper place to worship. And on and on it went. But no Jew with a brain in his head would consider that a Samaritan ten miles away or ten feet away was a neighbor worthy of decent treatment. They were the McCoys to Israel's Hatfields.

And now Jesus launches into His story. We pick up the action in verse 30: "A man was going down from Jerusalem to Jericho, when he fell into the hands of robbers. They stripped him of his clothes, beat him and went away, leaving him half dead."

This road is the famous, or infamous, *Wâdî Qelt*, which ran 17 miles from Jerusalem, 2,500 feet above sea level, down to Jericho, at 800 feet below. So it was a rocky, down-down-down journey, with plenty of places for Jesse James' gang to hide out. In fact, this particular area, this ravine, was openly called the "Valley of Blood." And that's how it works out here for this anonymous crime victim. Then Jesus continues:

"A priest happened to be going down the same road, and when he saw the man, he passed by on the other side. So too, a Levite, when he came to the place and saw him, passed by on the other side."

These two men, obviously, were operating under the "neighbor policy" of the day. "If I don't know you, forget it. Let the next guy dial 911, while I look out for Number One."

And now comes the punch line to the story. "But a Samaritan, as he traveled, came where the man was; and when he saw him, he took pity on him. He went to him and bandaged his wounds, pouring on oil and wine. Then he put the man on his own donkey, took him to an inn and took care of him. The next day he took out two silver coins and gave them to the innkeeper. 'Look after him,' he said, 'and when I return, I will reimburse you for any extra expense you may have.'"

End of story. And Jesus takes a deep breath. Everyone in the crowd, kind of mad about the ending, takes a breath too, and then rumbles a bit to the person standing next to them. "Stupid story. What's He mean?" And then Jesus leans in a bit to this lawyer. "Which of these men do you think was a neighbor to the man who fell into the hands of robbers?"

And the man couldn't bring himself to say the dreaded "S" word: "Samaritan." He just couldn't do it, even after a story like that. But he cleared his throat and reluctantly admitted: "Uh, the one who had mercy on him."

"You're right," Jesus said. And then these five archaic King James words which ring with such power still today: "Go, and do thou likewise."

23

THE SURPRISE DOUBLE-TWIST ENDING

If you ever thought you had a neighbor that even the best Christian shouldn't be expected to love, then consider this story. On June 10, 1942, Nazi German troops stormed into a town belonging to their Czechoslovakian neighbors. The village of Lidice had something like 500 inhabitants. And the Nazis lined up the men and executed, in cold blood, every single one of them. Just mowed them down. It was one of the worst atrocities of all of World War II.

The Nazis then burned down every house in the village and departed the women and children to Germany for "re-education." Even today, Lidice Memorial Day is observed on June 10 each year in New Jersey, as people remember the rape of this innocent town.

Suppose you could find a survivor still alive, maybe an old woman who was just a pale-faced, frightened child there in Lidice, and who saw her own father gunned down in that execution? Could you ask her, even today, to turn around and consider the Germans her neighbors? Can the people of God not only love the people who have historically not been our neighbors, but also go the second and third and fourth miles and learn to treat as neighbors those who have been decidedly un-neighborly towards us?

This story in Luke 10 is not only hard because of its ending, but made even harder because it turns into a call to action. Just as this good Samaritan was a good neighbor, Jesus then looks into the face of the questioning lawyer, and through the pages of Scripture into my face and your face, and gives us this command: "Go, and do thou likewise."

But is this Nazi story, "The Rape of Lidice," a proper application? How wide does Jesus Christ draw this circle, when we ask: "Who is my neighbor"?

Admittedly the animosity, the hatred, between Jews and Samaritans rose to this level of "Nazis vs. Czechs." These two groups hated each other, despised each other. These emotions started, of course, with nationalistic pride, and then went downhill from there. In the *Tyndale New Testament Commentaries* for Luke, author Leon Morris addresses this question of "Who is my neighbor"?

"There were different ideas among the Jews on this point, but they all seem to be confined to the nation Israel; the idea of love towards mankind had not reached them."

And the hated Samaritans, of course, were right there among them: always in their faces, always worshiping wrong, talking wrong, looking wrong, smelling wrong. Of course, the Samaritans felt the same way coming back. This war ran on both sides of the street, to be sure. Samaritans would never give Jews any shelter during their three-day trips from Galilee to Jerusalem. So travelers would have to take the long way around, going on the east side of the Jordan to avoid going through what they honestly considered to be enemy territory. And here in Luke 10, Jesus tells this parable which takes His listeners right into the heart of their own very worst hatred and prejudices and fears.

If you've ever listened to a story, and thought that you were one step ahead of the storyteller, and could see where this thing was going, that was probably the experience of this listening crowd. I mean, these things have a kind of rhythm to them, a one — two — three building up of the plot. And commentator Leon Morris suggests that the crowd very likely began to look ahead as Jesus tells the story. "All right," they think to themselves, "the priest doesn't stop to help. That pompous, overpaid . . . windbag, that Pharisee. And the Levite — he's a temple servant, and he doesn't stop either. So the big-shot church men don't stop to help. Well, just a regular guy, a common ordinary, blue-collar, fisherman Jew will probably come along next, and he'll be the man who stops to help. Ha!

I've figured it out ahead of time."

And you know, that would have been a not-half-bad parable. I could probably get a week of radio programs just out of that! But with the whole crowd thinking that a regular good guy is going to come along and save the day for Hollywood, Jesus throws them the most unexpected curve in the world. It is totally and completely un-anticipated when He says in verse 33: "But a Samaritan, as he traveled, came where the man was; and when he saw him, he took pity on him. He went to him and bandaged his wounds, pouring on oil and wine."

And that had to completely freak the crowd out. "What?! A Samaritan?" That plot twist hit them right in the guts. "Jesus, what are You talking about? You lost us right there." Not one of them saw that as a possible ending to this story.

Some of the others in the crowd, also self-proclaimed experts at guessing the punch line, probably expected that after the priest and the Levite came by, a villain was going to be next. In fact, the *International Bible Commentary* with noted theologian F. F. Bruce, makes that very suggestion: "A surprising *dénouement* (or Hollywood ending) to the story; 'the hearers would assume that the villain of the piece had arrived on the scene.'"

So, no, Jesus didn't give them the expected bad guy. And He didn't give them the good guy they had anticipated. To this crowd of Jews, He gave them a Samaritan. If it was citizens of Czechoslovakia, He'd have given them a Nazi. To a group of Ku Klux Klaners, a black businessman. To the Crips, a member of the Bloods. To a devout, family-values kind of church leader, a homosexual activist.

And as you think about this story and what it ought to mean in your life, think of the kind of person — or maybe the very exact person — you would struggle most of all to consider as a neighbor. And then have that person come along as Traveler #3 in this story.

Or turn it around: make that enemy the bleeding, half-dead victim . . . and *you* are Traveler #3. Because Jesus Christ tells this story to punch holes in every prejudice we've ever held, every grudge we've ever nurtured.

Speaking of grudges, do you know that this story about neighbors actually springs from a biblical lesson on the bearing of grudges? When the young lawyer, back in verse 25, asks Jesus, "What must I do to inherit eternal life?", Jesus lets him answer his own question. And the questioner correctly quotes from Leviticus 19:18 about loving your neighbor. But here's the full verse: "Do not seek revenge or bear a grudge against one of your people, but love your neighbor as yourself."

Isn't that interesting? Maybe a hard kind of interesting. Because Jesus is telling us here that not only does our racism and our prejudice have to go, but also our resentments and our grudges. That person whose behavior just bugs you to death . . . is your neighbor. The man you've steamed about privately for years . . . is your neighbor. That boss, that hypocrite in the church, that person who took you to court . . . is your neighbor. And in this story, it's that very person who is lying by the side of the road bleeding and half-dead, and you are Traveler #3 coming down from Jerusalem to Jericho.

Maybe you say — as I am very tempted to say as well — "I don't want that role. I could never love that person; no way. I could never be a neighbor to So-and-So." What's more, you might think in your heart (and be right about the fact) that if the tables were reversed, and you were lying in the dust, that enemy would never help you. Am I right? It's interesting to note, in another commentary book, entitled *The Desire of Ages*, that the author makes the very same point about this exact story. The traveling Samaritan comes down the road and sees this wounded Jew. And here's E. G. White's observation: "He [the Samaritan] did not question whether the stranger was a Jew or a Gentile. If a Jew, the

Samaritan well knew that, were their condition reversed, the man would spit in his face and pass him by with contempt." And he still gets off his donkey and helps his worst enemy.

Well, this is where we are. Can we be a neighbor to someone who not only doesn't treat us like a neighbor, but never will? Can we repay evil with good . . . even when we keep getting evil thrown in our faces? You know, Jesus submitted to the cross, and He prayed for the Roman soldiers who were driving nails through His hands. He prayed out loud for them. But when they heard that prayer, were their hearts touched? Did they repent? Did they pull out the nails and say they were sorry? No, they just kept on pounding those spikes. But Jesus continued to love them. He continued to demonstrate the most neighborly moment this universe has ever witnessed.

Aren't you glad for a Neighbor like that? And wouldn't you like to be one?

24

THE BEST ENEMY I EVER HAD

A church bulletin in Australia contributed the following litany to the delightful book, *More Holy Humor*, compiled by Cal and Rose Samra. It's entitled "The Pit," and has some lessons relating to this parable told by Jesus about the Good Samaritan.

"A man fell into a pit and couldn't get himself out." That's the premise of this particular dilemma. Okay, now here come all the helpers:

A *subjective* person came along and said, "I feel for you down there."

An *objective* person walked by and said, "It's logical that someone would fall down there."

A *Pharisee* said, "Only bad people fall into pits."

A *mathematician* calculated how he fell into the pit.

A *news reporter* wanted the exclusive story on the pit.

An *IRS agent* asked if he was paying taxes on the pit.

A *self-pitying person* said, "You haven't seen anything until you've seen my pit!"

A *fire-and-brimstone preacher* said, "You deserve your pit."

A *psychologist* noted, "Your mother and father are to blame for your being in that pit."

A *self-esteem therapist* said, "Believe in yourself and you can get out of that pit."

An *optimist* said, "Things could be worse."

A *pessimist* claimed, "Things *will* get worse."

And then here's the final entry: "Jesus, seeing the man, took him by the hand and lifted him out of the pit."

*   *   *

That's good, isn't it? But maybe we all saw ourselves elsewhere in this story, standing over the pit and calculating the trajectory of the person as he fell in, or a Sunday School teacher charting how many bad words the victim said while he was down there, or a dietician using a calorie chart to figure out how long before this poor guy starves to death. And then Jesus, without asking how he got there, or what mistakes he made to trip and fall in, just reaches down and pulls him out.

For about the past 15 years or so, there's been a cloud out there we call AIDS. The HIV virus. And every time it's announced on television or over the AP and UPI news wires that a certain celebrity is infected, the question comes up immediately: "How'd he get it? What did he do?" And there's this discussion and this pecking order of descending acceptability, starting with an innocent child who gets it from his mother. And the person who gets it from a blood transfusion. Down from there, there's the person who gets HIV from a spouse who cheated. Then the one who got it trading dirty needles. And then below that is the person who was promiscuous, but only in a heterosexual sense. And then last, and certainly least as well, the person who gets AIDS from rampant homosexual activity.

But here we see a Jesus, a Savior, who puts off discussions about who was worse than who, and simply pulls the helpless person out of the pit.

In the parable of the Good Samaritan, the helpless victim isn't in a pit; he's lying bleeding by the roadside. But he is equally helpless. He can't do anything to get himself to an inn or a hospital or an urgent care center. If he's going to be rescued, someone else is going to have to do it.

And if we ever had a lesson to learn in life, it's that we are that helpless victim! Maybe we traveled purposely down that road where we knew full well there were pitfalls. That 17-mile stretch between Jerusalem and Jericho, or for us it might be a moral Sodom and Gomorrah with the bars and brothels and bandits. We knew Satan and his band were down there in the rocks, but we took a chance. We went onto his territory. And sure enough, he attacked us and left us for dead.

There's not a one of us who can get to a hospital on our own. We haven't got money for the ambulance; we haven't even got a cell phone to dial 911, except for maybe the long-distance miracle of prayer. But in terms of sin and slavery to sin, every one of us is not just wounded on the road, but fatally wounded.

Maybe that statement doesn't seem real to you today. "I'm not helpless," you say. "I'm not even wounded. Not a scratch. I'm doing fine." Believe me when I say that we've gotten enough mail here at the Voice of Prophecy to demonstrate that all of us, sooner or later, are going to run into that nest of thieves. In terms of sin and righteousness, the realization of the human race's condition may not have hit you yet like it's hit so many others out there in our Radio Land . . . but it's coming. Without a Savior coming along, I'm a lost person and you're a lost person. There's a tough little verse back in Isaiah 41:24, which says this: "But you are less than nothing and your works are utterly worthless."

God doesn't say that to hurt our feelings or to drive us down — except onto our knees — but He does lovingly tell us how things are. We're wounded and we're bleeding and we're helpless. Unless the right person comes along after us, we're doomed.

And then comes this third Traveler. After the priest goes by and the Levite goes by, here comes the Samaritan. In this beautiful story, the life-saving assistance comes from the fallen man's worst enemy: the dreaded and despised Samaritan. And again maybe you scratch your head to follow the logic. You don't consider Jesus Christ to be your enemy. And yet in terms of the human race and its response to God and His Son Jesus, we certainly have treated Christ as an enemy, haven't we? He was an outcast when He came here. "My kingdom is not of this world," He told people. And just as Jews of that era might have wanted to ignore and insult and push and shove and spit on and kill Samaritans, they did all of that and more to this third Traveler, this visitor, this alien who had come to rescue them.

As we read through the details of this rescue, we get such a glimpse of the heart of Jesus. It says in verse 33 of the Samaritan: "He took pity on him." It was for pity and love that Christ came down here. He may have been an enemy to us, but we were never that to Him. He was moved by pity then, and He's still moved by pity now. As you bleed by the road, He's moved by pity and He's also moved to action.

Here's verse 34: "He went to him and bandaged his wounds, pouring on oil and wine. Then he put the man on his own donkey, took him to an inn and took care of him."

Notice that the bleeding man is placed on the rescuer's own donkey. The Samaritan walks while the victim rides. And when Jesus rescues, He gives us His own ride, so to speak. We get the benefits of His holiness while He walks the painful road to Calvary in our place.

The story continues in verse 35: "The next day he took out two silver coins and gave them to the innkeeper. 'Look after him,' he said, 'and when I return, I will reimburse you for any extra expense you may have.'"

Do we find any parallels even here? We certainly find a picture of ongoing assistance, of continued relationship. This good Samaritan paid the bill for right then, and he also provided for the long-term care of this wounded man, this enemy. Two silver coins, two denarii, back in those Bible times, would have been two days' salary. Which gives us a picture of a substantial gift, especially offered on behalf of a stranger and an enemy. Today it would be like paying maybe a couple hundred dollars' worth of someone's medical bills at the E.R.

According to the historian Polybius, those two silver coins, the average wages for two days, was sufficient, on the other hand, to provide for lodging in an inn like this for perhaps a couple of months. And we see here in the Scriptural story that he says to the innkeeper: "Take care of this man for me. Do whatever it takes. And if necessary, there's more where it came from. I'll reimburse you in full when I return."

You see, in the Christian faith Jesus' providence for us doesn't end on a hill called Calvary. That was a magnificent, noble rescue, but then we also see those two coins come out of the purse. And we receive continued, continuous healing from our Savior. He continues to be, in every sense of the word, a SAVIOR. As we continue to fall and as we sometimes fail to trust in Him, He picks us up. He forgives. He answers prayer. His arms are always open wide. He gives us, through the Holy Spirit, guidance in our daily life choices.

I hope that, even if it's in a small way, this radio ministry, The Voice of Prophecy, can be part of that expression of the two coins. Maybe you were saved many years ago, when you prayed the sinner's prayer and accepted Jesus as your Savior. That was the day Christ came along that Jericho road and picked you up, bound up your wounds, and carried you to the inn. But now, as the months and years go by, as you keep on healing, keep on growing, maybe He reaches out to you through our daily 15-minute messages and

gives you continued medical help. Medicine for the soul, that is.
Well, all the glory goes to Jesus, of course. And as I think about
this enemy, this Samaritan, and who he represents, there's a line
I've always wanted to twist around and use in a new way. Here it
is:

"With an enemy like that, who needs friends?"

25
OWNERS OF A HOTEL FRANCHISE

When the Voice of Prophecy first aired this "Parables" radio series, some of our listeners who had an emotional connection to that beautiful island country, the Philippines, found a special meaning in this chapter segment. Because it was *being* broadcast on a very special day for them: June 12, 1998, the 100th anniversary of that nation's independence. A century earlier, the Philippines declared its independence from Spain. Emilio Aguinaldo, the leader of insurgent rebel forces, was able to capitalize on the fact that Spain was weakened during the brief Spanish-American war of 1898, return from exile in Hong Kong, and declare an independent Philippine republic.

And in considering this marvelous Bible story, the parable of the Good Samaritan, that 100th anniversary kind of works for me. I think back to 1996, when our Voice of Prophecy team was over in the Philippines working on and celebrating TARGET 50,000 where God's people reached that many new members, fifty thousand, for His kingdom. And a number of great heroes come to mind.

Just one of many would be a local Seventh-day Adventist pastor named Virgilio Sabagai, who single-handedly nurtures, not two or three or five, but seventeen Christian churches. That's right! All by himself he is taking care of two thousand believers in 17 far-flung, spread-out congregations. And he gets from one church to the next on an old, cranky, beat-up twenty-year-old motorcycle. For how much pay? Two hundred dollars a month.

Now where does a hero like this one fit into Jesus' parable? Because we always like to place ourselves in the proper role in the closing credits. Of course, every citizen of this planet — pastors and popes and prostitutes alike — is the wounded victim by the side of the road. We all need rescue; we've all received the tender ministrations of the Great Physician, the Roadside Healer.

But then there's the application which is actually primary in this story. Because Jesus is talking here about *being* a good neighbor. And in this parable, it was the Good Samaritan who did that. The Good Samaritan helped his enemy; he was the one who swept aside prejudices and ancient hatreds and grudges and took a wounded foe to the inn and cared for him all night. And in the final credits, as Jesus gives that surprise ending, He then takes in the whole crowd in His direct gaze as He addresses the lawyer: "Which of these three do you think was a neighbor to the man who fell into the hands of robbers?"

And when the lawyer, the questioner, replied, reluctantly, "The one who had mercy on him," Jesus very clearly places a responsibility on the shoulders of every single follower in His kingdom: "Go, and do thou likewise." In the Living Bible: "Yes, now go and do the same."

Maybe you're a bit like me — and you think of an excuse, a loophole. "But, Lord, I'm so busy." "No," He says. "Go and do the same." "But . . . but . . . that person mistreated me! I've got a record of it in a file drawer back home!" "That doesn't matter," Jesus says. "Go and do the same." "But that's not my gift! I'm not a good people person. I'm shy. I'd rather contribute to the church and let the deacons and deaconesses help the hurting man in the street." And our Savior says in response to every excuse — yours and mine both: "No, My child. This isn't a role for just a few. This isn't an elected position for the very elect. If you're part of My kingdom, My heavenly entourage, then this is how it's going to be. As the Good Samaritan did in My story, go, and do thou likewise." There's nothing soft or vague about these parables; they're not Hallmark card bedtime stories, but real, gritty do-it-now spiritual challenges.

In the text notes from the New International Version, the Bible scholars comment where Jesus asks the question: "Which of these three men was the good neighbor?" Here's their own query:

"Who proves he is the good neighbor by his actions?" Because the Word of God calls us to a faith that is active, a faith that is proven to be legitimate and real by its actions.

Especially in the book of James, but here as well, we find a two-thousand-year-old expression of the old adage that "talk is cheap." "Do you really love your neighbor as yourself?" Jesus asks. "There's someone wounded and bleeding in your path. Maybe someone you don't like. Someone you've looked down on or resented or hated. Now is the time to show if you're a good neighbor, the kind of good neighbor who will be in God's kingdom." Maybe you recall this line from I John 2:6: "He that saith he abideth in Him [Jesus] ought himself also to walk, even as He walked."

Now, what do those King James words mean? How did Jesus walk? Well, He walked with a lot of pauses and stops. When someone was hurting, He stopped and helped. When someone was crying, He stopped and dried their tears. When even an enemy was shouting at Him from the sidewalk, Christ paused and reached out to reconcile, to forgive and heal. And if we want to walk as Jesus walked, we have to pause where He paused, and stop where He stopped.

In the great old 19th-century classic on the life of Jesus, entitled *The Desire of Ages*, Ellen White beautifully explores this very Bible story: the Good Samaritan. And then she addresses the issue of "talk is cheap." Notice:

"The lesson is no less needed in the world today than when it fell from the lips of Jesus. Selfishness and cold formality have well-nigh extinguished the fire of love, and dispelled the graces that should make fragrant the character. Many who profess His name have lost sight of the fact that Christians are to represent Christ. Unless there is practical self-sacrifice for the good of others, in the family circle, in the neighborhood, in the church, and wherever we may be, then whatever our profession, we are not Christians."

I remember the first time I noticed that last line. Unless we practice self-sacrifice "for the good of others" — not just in our homes and in our own neighborhoods, and in our own home churches, but everywhere — then it doesn't really matter what we say with our lips. I can be the established writer and producer for The Voice of Prophecy and part-time pastor at the Ojai Valley Adventist Church. But those are just words. If I don't sacrifice like the Good Samaritan did, if I don't love people as this paragraph says, "wherever I may be," then my profession of the Christian faith means nothing. Listen, this is a big story! If you're looking for the skid marks where the rubber is supposed to meet the road, then you've just found them and so have I.

And if you want biblical proof for this concept, look no further than chapter four of First John, which is about this from start to finish. Here it is nailed down in verse 20: "If anyone says, 'I love God,' yet hates his brother, he is a liar." And then the chapter concludes with this: "And He has given us this command: Whoever loves God must also love his brother."

So as we assign roles in this dramatic story, you and I are the victim. But we're also that Good Samaritan . . . at least we are if we want to be a part of God's kingdom.

But as we close and move to Parable #6, can we even find a third role for ourselves? Notice that when the Good Samaritan had bound up the wounds and lifted the man onto his own donkey, he took him to an inn and asked the innkeeper to care for him until he should return. He provided the innkeeper with resources — those two silver coins. "Take care of him," he instructed. "If you need more money later, I'll provide that too. But until I get back, I'm putting this man in your care."

So let me suggest that all of us in the Christian faith have now been made innkeepers as well! Because Jesus, the Great Rescuer, the greatest Samaritan of them all, has picked up many wounded and broken people. Where does He take them? To the church. The church is the hospital for desperate sinners, for those who are bleeding with problems and pain. And He says to those in the Church: "I have to leave for a while. But here are resources — spiritual gifts and talents and blessings. If you need more, My Holy Spirit will provide them too. But look after this friend of Mine until I return."

Some of these victims He brings are lonely or sad or emotionally wounded. But sometimes they're just sinners: bad people who do bad things. Listen, people need rescue from sin more than from any other disease. More than from bullet wounds caused by drive-by shootings. And the Good Samaritan says to the innkeepers in the Church: "Take care of this person. I'll be back soon, and in the meantime, I'll provide the resources."

In that same book, *The Desire of Ages*, is another jewel of a para-graph, despite its 19th-century style. "By faith and prayer press back the power of the enemy. Speak words of faith and courage that will be as a healing balsam to the bruised and wounded one. Many, many, have fainted and become discouraged in the great struggle of life, when one word of kindly cheer would have strengthened them to overcome. Never should we pass by one suf-fering soul without seeking to impart to him of the comfort where-with we are comforted of God."

Back to the Philippines and our motorcycle pastor, Virgilio Sabagai. I guess he's not just a country preacher, but now, Jesus says, the head of a great lodging chain — with 17 hotels. And the message on his letterhead, directed at you and at me: "Go, and do thou likewise."

The Senseless Software King

26
HOW TO SPEND A BILLION

He drove one of those chocolate-brown delivery trucks part-time
for UPS. Thirty hours a week, no benefits. High school diploma,
one semester of community college. But Jared had dropped out
after the Christmas break with two B's and a C. It wasn't worth
paying even the 13 bucks per unit for J.C. credits — junior college — if he just wasn't into it. So he spent his free time hacking
around with his computer and talking software with his two
friends.

For some reason, computers was something Jared could do. He
was always breaking into the program part of various games, and
tweaking the speeds of the cursor or the erratic bounce of the little
"Jezz balls." In fact, ever since dropping out of college, he'd been
trying to create a kind of landscape game, something like the
Internet Dungeons and Dragons, but with more funk to it, more
real options. He and his two friends would sit around until two
a.m. guzzling whole cases of diet Coke and brainstorming ways to
create their own Cyberspace world where game players could log
on and just go and go and go endlessly.

And finally one night, Jared said to the others: "Look, you nuts.
Let's just go for it. Let's do it. " He'd stacked up around three
thousand dollars from the UPS route; the other two guys each had
some cash to put in. In fact, Jared had a VISA gold card he'd
never used much, and it had a ten-thousand dollar limit he could
tap. So the three guys actually sat down one long weekend and
began mapping out the software game. They spent four thousand
dollars to contract out some of the graphic tricks — even though
Jared tinkered around so much with the consultant's designs that
the other two complained that they shouldn't even pay for the outside help.

And finally, when it was ready to show someone, Steve, who had a friend in Silicon Valley that specialized in Internet access entertainment, set up a pitch meeting. Before they knew it, they were right in the middle of an IPO — Wall Street slang for an "Initial Public Offering," where stocks are sold to fund a new company. "Man, this is kind of wild," Jared said to his buddies as they signed sheet after sheet of contracts and codicils and corporate agreements. "I may not have time to stay with the UPS people anymore if this thing takes off on us."

Well, about a week and a half went by, and then one morning the phone rang. Jared had overslept and it took him about five rings to get to the receiver. It was Steve. "Did you hear the news?" And his friend was almost screaming into his ear. "No, what?" He was still kind of half-asleep. But then Steve shouted it into his brain: "We're all billionaires!"

"What? Huh? We're millionaires? What are you talking about, man?"

"No! Billionaires. Starting with a 'B'! Billionaires! The IPO just took off. It hit Wall Street like a rocket and they already had to split it. That's a billion three for me and for you and for Paco. And it's still going up. Some guy on CNBC was just saying it might double again before they close tonight. We're stinking filthy rich!!"

Jared hung up the phone almost shaking in his pajama bottoms. He was a billionaire? As in a one with nine zeroes after it? He glanced at his watch. Eight forty-five. He was supposed to be on the UPS truck in 15 minutes, delivering packages and earning a grand total of $9.45 an hour. For a second, the incongruous thought crossed his mind: should he show up for work to drive the truck or to buy out the company? He — Jared McKnight — at the age of 19, was worth 1.3 billion dollars.

Well, if there was ever a week of Voice of Prophecy radio programs designed to depress everyone on the outside looking in, I guess this would be that week. Because stories like the above, this fictional kid named Jared, are happening all the time around us now. All up and down the street, we're living next door to people who are instant millionaires. And once in a while, you can put a "B' in there instead and admit: "My next-door neighbor — not me, but my next-door neighbor — is a bonafide billionaire."

During the long bull run of the 1990s, Wall Street turned more and more people into millionaires overnight. The April 27, 1998 issue of *Newsweek* had a cover story entitled "Married to the Market." And it showed a picture of a 57-year-old man named David Meyers; the editors called him a "poster child for the roaring market of the '90s." He was planning to slog along until he was 65 or even older, earning a paycheck from his Colgate-Palmolive factory job. But his retirement accounts have done so well, just roaring right through the roof, that he's been able to quit early. Now he stays home and plays with his antique phonograph collection, saying to himself every morning when he wakes up: "Thank you, Dow Jones, Nasdaq, and S&P."

There's a story in the book of Luke describing the bull market of Jesus' day. Which back then, of course, involved real bulls! The stock traders "in the pits" really were in the pits, dealing in sheep futures and selling short in the dates market and staking out a position on camel-hair coats. And here in chapter 12, Jesus describes the wildly successful portfolio of a gentleman farmer.

"The ground of a certain rich man produced a good crop. He thought to himself, 'What shall I do? I have no place to store my crops.' Then he said, 'This is what I'll do. I will tear down my barns and build bigger ones, and there I will store all my grain and my goods. And I'll say to myself, "You have plenty of good things laid up for many years. Take life easy; eat, drink and be merry."'"

It's interesting that the more things change, the more they stay the

same, don't they? All through the history of this world, there have
been those people who had the dilemma of too much money. I
mean, this man literally cannot deal with the fact of how rich he is.
He can't spend the money he has. He faces Bill Gates' dilemma
— not being able to spend his money fast enough. There isn't
room for all the cars he could buy, the houses, the boats, the caviar,
the indoor pools, the art collections, the personal home movie the-
aters.

I recall a story going back to the 1960s, where even a person with
a lowly million bucks could create a stir and make people jealous.
But even back then, Elizabeth Taylor couldn't spend the money as
fast as it came in. According to the gossip columnists, the help at
her mansion would put new sheets on her bed every night. Not
newly laundered sheets — *new* sheets. They would be used exactly once, fresh from the most exotic silk-sheet factories, and then
discarded or given away. New sheets slept in exactly one time,
and this was how she treated herself 365 days a year. Why?
Simply to use up at least some of her money.

And here in this Bible story, the central character faces this happy
dilemma. How can I store these crops? How can I possibly spend
this much money? Help!

Well, all of us looking on from the sidelines as Wall Street breaks
the 10,000 barrier without us, and as Microsoft splits and splits and
splits again, creating more and more billionaires, wish we had this
problem. But in the Bible story, the rich man doesn't come to a
very positive end. Let's pick up the rest of the story, beginning
now in verse 20, right after the "eat, drink and be merry" part.
"But God said to [the rich man]: 'You fool! This very night your
life will be demanded from you. Then who will get what you have
prepared for yourself?'" And then Christ concludes, speaking to all
of us: "This is how it will be with anyone who stores up things for
himself but is not rich toward God.

End of story. That very night the billionaire dies, and the same God who tells us to be gentle and tender in our speech, thunders at this particular man: "You're a fool! You're going to die tonight, fella! Who's going to drive your Rolls-Royces then? Who's going to wear your Armani suits and live in your 24-bedroom, 22-bathroom, sunken-tub in the master suite, eight fireplaces, nine-car garage mansion? Not you; that's for sure . . . because the angel of death is going to come calling tonight before midnight."

What do we make of a story like this one, with its abrupt swing from bull market to bear, from good news to bad, from delirious joy to disaster and death?

You know, the Bible never says it's a sin to have a good crop. There's nothing wrong with tearing down a little barn and upgrading to a bigger one. It's not wrong to store your crops for a rainy day. It's not against God's law to eat, or to drink, or even to enjoy the right kind of merriment. Even Jesus went to parties. But if we read verse 21, it's absolutely disastrous to be rich — in old Judea or in today's Silicon Valley or Wall Street or sitting down to lunch at Beverly Hills' exclusive El Carmen Café for a pitch meeting with your agent and a couple of dealmakers from MTV — if you're not also "rich toward God."

But how does Jesus defines that intriguing expression?

27
MAKING A KILLING ON THE DODGERS

It probably seemed like a big purchase back in 1950, a major-league expenditure if you'll pardon the pun. Because that's exactly what it was when Mr. Walter O'Malley bought from the famous Branch Rickey a franchise then known as the Brooklyn Dodgers. It cost him $1.5 million to pay for "them bums," as the lovable but ball-dropping team was called there in New York City.

Now, nearly a half-century later, as everyone in the sports world knows, Peter O'Malley turned around and sold the same team, now the L.A. Dodgers, to Rupert Murdoch's Fox Group for a cool $311 million . . . by far and away the highest price ever paid for a team in any sport, anywhere, anytime. And yes, that's a 21,000% profit on the original investment. Not bad for 48 years of what most of us would consider a dream job: owning a baseball team.

And then we move into the question under discussion here: what is it appropriate to do with that kind of nest egg? That's a whole Dodger Stadium full of cash! $311 million is a lot of Dodger Dogs and many, many nights sitting in a luxury box right over home plate. Is it wrong to hoard the money? Is it wrong to stash it away so that the O'Malley name will always be a dynasty in sports, wielding power and clout right into the 21st and 22nd centuries?

Here in Luke 12, as we study a parable we're calling "The Senseless Software King," it doesn't appear that the rich man in question did anything wrong except for one mistake. He got rich on a lucky break, which is certainly all right to do. He upgraded his operation; that's acceptable too: tearing down small barns and building bigger ones. He planned for himself a life of ease — not much different from what every retiree in the world dreams about. But God said to the rich farmer with the bulging barns: "You fool! You're going to die tonight . . . and then what? You stored up things for yourself, but were not 'rich toward God.'"

Again, it's quite helpful to read the entire chapter where a particular story is told. Luke 12 actually has about six sections to it, at least as divided in some Bibles. And it says right in verse 1: "Meanwhile, when a crowd of many thousands had gathered, so that they were trampling on one another, Jesus began to speak first to His disciples."

Here's a little hidden point. Jesus was a popular speaker and teacher. Thousands were hanging on His every word. He had followers and devotees and people of means who wanted to subscribe to His monthly newsletter, so to speak. We could easily assume that if Christ had wanted to pursue worldly wealth and amass a temporal fortune, He could have done that. He could have taken up big offerings and lived in comfort, just working His miracles, appearing as a guest on the Trinity cable network, and publishing a Zondervan bestseller every year or two. And so when He talks about the dangers of wealth, and the perspectives that a person blessed by God should hold to, we can take those words seriously.

Then as we study through this chapter, looking at these several subsections, we find some interesting clues. We're especially interested, of course, in what Christ might mean by that phrase: "being rich toward God." Again, Jesus doesn't teach that it's wrong to prosper. It's not wrong to invest for tomorrow, and it's not a sin to enjoy some years of comfort and leisure after decades of hard work. It's not even wrong to "luck into" a big fortune; Christ told other parables where people did exactly that. But this is a vital warning — to remain in an attitude of being "rich toward God."

In the first 12 verses, Christ talks about not being afraid of a person's enemies. "If My Father doesn't even forget the little sparrow," He says, "He for sure won't forget to protect you." But then notice this in verse 8: "I tell you, whoever acknowledges Me before men, the Son of Man will also acknowledge him before the angels of heaven."

So whether you and I are poor or fabulously wealthy, here's a necessary ingredient in a person's life: a willingness to acknowledge
Jesus Christ. To say publicly before others: "I'm committed to
Christ. I belong to Him." In fact, you might safely become a millionaire, even a multi-millionaire . . . but only as long as you are
willing to say on *Larry King* or when they interview you for
Money magazine: "Jesus Christ is my Lord; I owe my first alle-
giance to Him."

Apparently in this story, there was no such acknowledging. Very
clearly this man, as he tore down barns and built bigger ones, was
saying to himself: "I will trust in THIS. This fortune right here is
my security and my future."

In this haughty little diatribe of boasting, we notice one word four
times: "What shall I do? I have no place to store MY crops." And
then he decides: "I will tear down MY barns and build bigger ones,
and there I will store all MY grain and MY goods."

A very wealthy man was also a dedicated born-again believer. And
he had a house that was filled with nice things, expensive furnish-
ings. How did he keep from worshiping those things, from trusting in his money? a fellow Christian once asked. "I mentally have
put a little sticker on every single thing I own," the man admitted.
"What does the sticker say?" And he replied: "Soon to be burned."
In other words, this man was acknowledging Jesus as his sustainer,
and heaven as his future home.

In the next section of Luke 12, Jesus talks about not worrying.
"Look at the birds of the field," He says. "Look at the lilies. They
don't worry about tomorrow, and My Father cares for them." And
again there is this theme: trusting in God for our security.

Acknowledging Him. In fact, it's right here in this section, part of
Luke 12, where we find the very famous bit of biblical advice:
"Provide purses for yourselves that will not wear out, a treasure in

heaven that will not be exhausted, where no thief comes near and no moth destroys. For where your treasure is, there your heart will be also."

This passage is referring to the Bible teaching that we should care for the poor among us. Which, of course, we can't do if we're worried and insecure and fixated on our own needs. But these verses are telling us the same consistent truth: our security, our identity, our first passion, is Jesus Christ. This attitude is one of being "rich toward God."

The next section in this wonderful Bible passage has this title in my Bible: "Watchfulness." And Jesus advises His listeners: "Be watching for the Master's coming. Be waiting for My return." Is it harder for a wealthy, successful person to be watching for Jesus to come? Harder, yes. Impossible, no. But it's a challenge to keep the Second Coming of Christ foremost in our thinking, especially if we're distracted by our goals and our possessions, and particularly if we're so satisfied with this life that we're not really that passionate about the next one.

Jesus also says, in verse 15: "Watch out! Be on your guard against all kinds of greed; a man's life does not consist in the abundance of his possessions."

So we need to watch for the coming of the Master. And we need to also watch for the coming of another master named Greed — as he rears his ugly head in our life. You look into your heart, and I'll look into mine. Is greed growing? Is a love for things and wealth and power and influence slowly but steadily asserting itself as a dominant force?

In his book *Living Faith*, President Jimmy Carter tells the story of Millard and Linda Fuller. Millard was a clever, inventive entrepreneur-type who just had everything he touched turn to gold. Even as a student as the University of Alabama, he was a money-maker.

He'd get bootleg copies of the student roster, figure out who had a birthday on what date, and then offer his services to parents back home as the go-between to get a cake and flowers delivered. This guy knew how to make money, and as a young married lawyer he began to do even better.

Except in one area: his marriage. Finally Linda told him that she was leaving him and returning home to New York. Well, he came to his senses and begged her and the family to stay with him. And he actually made this promise: "Honey, I'll give away all our money if you want me to and put away all of these projects of mine. And instead, I'll join you in any kind of work we can do together."

And that's exactly what they did. They joined a kind of Christian biracial commune there near Plains, Georgia, known as Koinonia Farm — *koinonia* being a Greek Bible word meaning "brother-hood." He spent five years there helping poor families build houses for themselves.

From there Millard and Linda Fuller began their own dream which they call Habitat For Humanity, an organization that helps under-privileged people all around the world get into affordable houses which they build themselves. Maybe you've heard of it; former President Carter serves on the board and actually puts on his blue jeans and travels around the globe perspiring and nailing and dry-walling right next to the excited people who are soon going to be moving in to these brand new, very modest but serviceable homes.

Get this: Habitat For Humanity, as of the 1996 publishing of Carter's book, had helped more than 50,000 needy families build and inhabit new homes in 1,500 communities in the United States and also in 41 countries around the world. Millard and Linda say that Habitat "uses the theology of the hammer." And I like their second description even better, because it gives such affirmation to this parable told by Christ. This is, they say, the "economics of Jesus."

28
WHO CAN STOP LEO NOW?

Something very rare happened quite recently, and all of us at the Voice of Prophecy are humbly proud about it. The *Voice of Prophecy News* is our ministry magazine, sent out free of charge to our many supporters and prayer partners around North America. And I will say, tongue in cheek, that this is one of the few magazines in 1998 to not have Mr. Leonardo DiCaprio on its cover. Despite "Leo's" meteoric rise to superstardom aboard the unsinkable hit, *Titanic*, we've put out just about the only magazine you can find that has come up with other things to feature.

And yet, in studying the story of the rich farmer, young Mr. DiCaprio's recent success gives us quite a bit to think about. Because just like the wealthy man in this Bible parable told by Christ, we have here a young star who quickly — well, actually, instantly — moved to the big leagues. He's gone from a $2 million actor to the stratosphere: $20 million is now his asking price per picture. Young Jack Dawson isn't going to have to sail the Atlantic in steerage ever again; he'll be in first class wearing his own tuxedo from now on, thank you very much. Being the lead star in the most successful motion picture ever made will do that for an aspiring actor.

There are a couple of important lessons, though, in this story, that are themselves "titanic" in their importance. The people on that great ship of 1912 learned it, certainly. And so should Leonardo DiCaprio and director James Cameron . . . and so should you and I. And that's this: there's no sure thing in life, if it's created by man. You probably remember the famous line assigned to "Titanic" — "God Himself could not sink this ship." But only a fool says what God can or cannot do.

Now, it wasn't God who sank the *Titanic*. But this great ocean liner, on its maiden voyage, was the closest thing there was to a sure thing. It was so safe they didn't bother with very many lifeboats. Things were so secure that the owners relaxed. Right up to the very last moment, people wouldn't get in the lifeboats because they thought that the *Titanic* was a sure thing. But Jesus tells us here in Luke 12 that nothing is sure in this world.

A successful farmer had scored his own kind of Hollywood hit. A huge cash crop had come in, and he was rolling in denarii; he couldn't tote his bags of cash to the Bank of Jerusalem fast enough. But he said to himself, "This is a sure thing. 'You have plenty of good things laid up for many years. Take life easy; eat, drink and be merry.'" But then as Christ relates this story to His many listeners, He added this warning about sure things: "But God said to him, 'You fool! This very night your life will be demanded from you. Then who will get what you have prepared for yourself?'"

There was an excellent article in the May 4, 1998 issue of *Newsweek*, featuring some of the ever-younger talent in Hollywood today. It was entitled "Moving in the Fast Lane," and described some of the kids who are now big players: writing, producing, directing. "All it takes is one good day in L.A. to change your life," said a young man, Matt Antrim, age 28, who moved from Kansas City to L.A., and landed a lucrative job with E! Entertainment Television in just 12 days. A fresh-faced kid named Mike Horowitz, just 23 years old, is all of a sudden the director of acquisitions for the Sundance Channel. He's got all the clout in the world, and confesses how insane it is that he's got so much power. Then he adds: "All of my friends, whether they're in the business [that's show business] or waiting tables or just hanging out, all believe they are a day away from being millionaires."

Well, that's all very heady stuff, but then I flipped over exactly one page, and here was a follow-up article in the same magazine with this chilling title: "So You Wanna Be a Star?" And it had this plummeting down-to-earth sidebar title: "Yes, you could be next

week's hot new actor. But look out. Your career might be over
before you can fill your swimming pool." And it tells how every
studio in town is out there right now looking for the next DiCaprio.
And one actress admitted: "If a star fades, it's like, 'OK, *next!*'"
Especially the pretty young female stars in town know that when
they hit the dreaded 40th birthday, it's over for them. Careers can
plummet and flame out like the candles on the cake.

So what do we do when we realize that fortunes can slip away —
or be abruptly snatched away by death, or the mere turn of a calen-
dar page? As Jesus Himself asks: "Then who will get what you
have prepared for yourself?" It's a sobering parallel that in this
story of *Titanic*, this terrible "Night to Remember," some 1500
people basically came to realize that they were going to die that
night. A few had false hopes, to be sure. But the sober among
them knew that with the 29-degree water, and with the nearest boat
so many miles away, they were minutes away from eternity. And
just as when God said to the rich man in the parable, "This night
your life will be required of you," that realization so abruptly
changes every value system. What things are important then?
What items do you put in your pockets as you go up on deck, and
what do you leave behind in your stateroom?

There are Bible verses which speak directly to this issue of false
values. Job 27:8 — and certainly this was a man who went
through trials designed to alter every human paradigm. Notice:
"For what hope has the godless when he is cut off, when God takes
away his life?"

Or Psalm 39:6: "Man is a mere phantom as he goes to and fro: He
bustles about, but only in vain." Now notice this: "He heaps up
wealth, not knowing who will get it."

Now, he may think he knows. Most of the world is brimming in
confidence about what it believes to be sure things. In November
of '97, when there was a scary, 554-point roller coaster drop in the

Dow, *Newsweek* magazine ran a reassuring cover article, and then this sidebar article entitled "What Should You Do?" And they included a little math chart which made this assertion: If you hold stocks over a one-year period, you stand a 26% chance of losing money. Over five years, it's just a 10% gamble. Hold on for ten years, and it's just four percent.

But get this: as Jane Bryant Quinn and the money experts in New York look over the landscape of the past, they make us this promise: if you hold onto your portfolio for at least 20 years, then the chance of a loss is ZERO. No chance at all! In other words, if you begin now and hang on to your stocks through the ups and the downs, two decades from now, they guarantee that you will have made money. In other words, this is a sure thing. It can't miss.

Well, let me say just one thing about that. Because I can tell you right now, at this very moment, when the stock market is not only going to crash, and dip down below 7,000 or 5,000 or even down to 2,000. I can tell you the day it's going to go clear back down to zero! And that's the day when Jesus Christ returns to this earth. Your portfolio and mine and the entire Dow Jones system, the Nikkei, the Hang Seng index and all the rest . . . are going to be completely flattened down to zero.

The kingdom of God is the only sure thing you and I can hold onto as we look at the world around us. Empires look so permanent until an earthquake hits. Fortunes appear to be invincible until an unexpected bear market melts away all the money. Someone looks like they just can't be stopped; they've got all the financial momentum in the world, until a shadow shows up on their X-ray. Even the fabulously wealthy Sir Paul, ex-Beatle Paul McCartney, worth hundreds of millions of dollars, found that all his money couldn't buy him love, couldn't keep his lovely Linda alive for even one more day beyond April 17, 1998, couldn't stave off the curse of breast cancer. Friend, nothing is sure in this world except Jesus.

I imagine that Major Arthur Peuchen thought that the tin box in his stateroom, C-104, was a sure thing on that cold Sunday night. In it he had $200,000 in bonds, and another $100,000 in preferred stocks. John Jacob Astor was a respected multimillionaire, with a portfolio nobody could touch. Benjamin Guggenheim, the tuxedo-clad tycoon, also with a fortune that couldn't be dented by a $4,350 ticket for a deluxe first-class suite. Mr. and Mrs. Isador Straus of Philadelphia had built a china business into an empire we still know today as Macy's. And their fortunes were secure as well, they thought. Nothing could take away the charity balls, the board appointments, the glitter of traveling on maiden voyages. All told, there was $250,000,000 worth of human fortune on board the great, unsinkable *Titanic* when she struck an iceberg at 41-40 North Latitude, 50-14 West Longitude, 11:40 in the evening on April 14, 1912.

29
WHEN UP IS REALLY DOWN

What do you do when it suddenly seems that every rule, every axiom, every principle you've had confidence in is suddenly wiped away?

There's a fascinating book, kind of a Christian science fiction allegory, entitled *Perelandra*, the middle book in a trilogy by the late, great C. S. Lewis. It's filled with strange and intriguing imagery of battles between good and evil, with invasions by Lucifer into a pure new world. But right at the outset of the story, Lewis writes himself briefly into the narrative, and is visiting his friend Elwin Ransom, the hero of the saga.

As he waits in the darkness of Ransom's little country cottage, terrified by the "hauntedness" of the place, desperately wishing his friend would arrive, he suddenly hears and almost sees one of the heavenly beings or *eldils*. You and I would say it was an angel. But right there in the room was this *thing*, this creature from beyond our world, that could speak and communicate.

But the interesting little point I want to borrow is this: somehow this creature had changed the geography of the place. Here's Lewis' own description: "It was not at right angles to the floor. . . . What one actually felt at the moment was that the column of light was vertical but the floor was not horizontal — the whole room seemed to have heeled over as if it were on board ship. The impression, however produced, was that this creature had reference to some horizontal, to some whole system of directions, based outside the Earth, and that its mere presence imposed that alien system on me and abolished the terrestrial horizontal."

Isn't that strange? This *eldil*, this angel, even without saying a word about it, seemed to bring into that cottage a whole different gravity. It hovered there above him, bringing the authority of heaven's "horizontal" and heaven's "vertical" into that little building in England; it imposed the geography of an alien kingdom on Lewis and Ransom. For that moment, at least, "up" was what God said was up, and not where you usually saw the ceiling and the chimney above you.

And here in this parable of Jesus, told to a huge crowd, it seems that the same thing has happened again. According to the "up" and the "down" and the "left" and the "right" of human wisdom, this gentleman farmer had made all the right moves. He had a big crop, and he cashed in on it. He stored up wealth for a rainy day. He tore down little barns and built bigger ones; he moved his funds from a savings account to a CD account, then into aggressive stocks, then into high-flying derivatives and offshore investments. He did exactly what his on-line internet broker told him to do. And this was all according to the wisdom of the world. Who among us today wouldn't play it that same way? But at the end of the story, Jesus paints a picture where God reaches down and tells this man: "You've done it all wrong. Every single move you've made is going to backfire because you're going to forfeit your life tonight." "This very night" are the exact three words Jesus uses.

I've used the expression several times: "upside-down math." Because in the kingdom of heaven, all of the former rules no longer apply! It would be as if "up" for the Dow Jones was the wrong direction. Breaking through the 10,000 barrier, and then the 11,000 would be bad news financially, making you poorer every night. Because as Jesus Christ tells this story, prosperity according to the measure of mankind ends up adding up to a big zero, especially when a man's life ends that very evening.

Clear back in the book of Deuteronomy Moses makes a long and impassioned speech to the Children of Israel, and he gets into some of this "upside-down math": "Be careful that you do not forget the Lord your God, failing to observe His commands, His laws and His decrees that I am giving you this day. Otherwise, when you eat and are satisfied, when you build fine houses and settle down, and when your herds and flocks grow large and your silver and gold increase and all you have is multiplied" — this is worldly math now, notice — "then your heart will become proud and you will forget the Lord your God, who brought you out of Egypt, out of the land of slavery. . . . You may say to yourself, 'My power and the strength of my hands have produced this wealth for me.' But remember the Lord your God, for it is He who gives you the ability to produce wealth."

We learn a lot here. One thing about this planet's geography and also its math is the concept that we get the credit for what we earned. The Israelites had this; did you notice? Saying to themselves: "My power and the strength of my hands have produced this wealth for me." But who had split the Red Sea for them? Who had led them out of Egypt and given them this fertile soil? The rich farmer in Jesus' story had this same misconception, thinking to himself: "I'm rich now. These are my crops, my bulging barns. I've done pretty well." And according to the world's math, he certainly had.

It was noted in a *Newsweek* report that, just in the first quarter of 1998, the rising tide of Wall Street had made Microsoft's Bill Gates $13 billion richer. Right behind him is Warren Buffett, who operates the high-flying Berkshire Hathaway fund, which has gone from a stock price of $18 per share in 1965 to its recent level of $70,500 per share. His yacht floated upward in the first three months of 1998 to the tune of $10 billion.

Again, what does the world say, once it chokes back the lump of envy in its throat? "Good for you. Lucky Bill and lucky Warren. The rich have just gotten richer." What does the upside-down math of heaven say? Two things, really. First of all, no man or woman should ever forget who gives us the power to earn. Secondly, no man or woman should ever forget, first and foremost, to become, as Jesus put it in this story, "rich toward God."

A person can, in a perfectly proper way, become wealthy. AND remain "right-side up" with heaven, as long as he or she keeps those two principles in mind. One, giving all honor to God. Two, remaining in a close, trusting, giving, depending relationship with that same God.

In the exceptional book *Descending Into Greatness*, Christian pastor Bill Hybels tells story after story of people who have discovered the arithmetic of heaven. I mean, just consider that title: *Descending Into Greatness*. People on Wall Street would fall over laughing if you even suggested those three words. Power brokers in Washington would shake their heads in dismay if you tried to give them a book with that on the cover. But over and over, the Word of God tells us that ascending into greater wealth, and ascending into circles of political influence, and ascending to higher levels of ego-stroking . . . can be a one-way trip to destruction.

And Hybels says this in a very personal way: "Although the idea of descending was and still is somewhat difficult to define, it clearly requires choice. Whatever it means, descending into greatness is the way of Jesus Christ. If we want to follow in the footsteps of the Son of God, we have to consciously move down."

He then tells his own story, because as a young man, he was part of a lucrative family business. The Hybels family was doing very well financially with a successful wholesale produce company in Kalamazoo, Michigan. And his own dad was pushing him up, up, up through the ranks. In seventh grade he was already going on solo sailing adventures on a 45-foot boat. He toured Africa and Europe alone for eight weeks as a 15-year-old. After just two years of college he was poised to take over the business and become a multimillionaire.

Then the Holy Spirit got hold of him, by way of a Christian summer camp director. And he asked him a question reminiscent of Christ's in this story: "Bill," he said, "what are you doing with your life that will last forever?"

Wow! That question haunted him. It dogged him day and night. Sure, in the world's eyes he was a kid on the fast-track. But what about being "rich toward God"? And so Bill Hybels left it all. He went to Chicago and began to work in ministry at minimum wage. He got into youth ministry and soon had a thousand kids worshiping at his Park Ridge church. And then God called him DOWN again, to what is now known as the Willow Creek Church.

Even today, he reports, the math of the world still beckons. Maybe a bigger salary. Television opportunities. Book royalties. Political connections. So that descending into greatness doesn't involve just one U-turn, but many of them. Time after time, he's had to fall on his knees and surrender any selfish desire, any clinging to the trappings of power.

Well, how is it with me? I can't tell Bill Gates what to do. But I can look deep into my own heart, using the flashlight of truth God's Holy Spirit is pleased to lend me. God help me to surrender my self-confidence, my insecure hoarding of wealth, my lifelong searchings for position. God help me to make my way DOWN, toward what heaven regards as greatness, toward what Jesus Himself describes as being "rich toward God."

30
HOW MUCH SHOULD AL HAVE TO GIVE?

It was a scathing rebuke from *Newsweek's* popular column, the "Conventional Wisdom Watch." A few years back it came leaking out about how much various politicians had contributed to charity during the prior tax year. And Vice President Gore came in for a great big down arrow for the week, and this jab: "Usually generous Al gives Grinchy $353 to charity. *Hello?* Aren't you running for prez?"

Aides for the vice president were quick to point out some much larger amounts in prior years: many tens of thousands of dollars given to charities, mostly from book royalties. But in this Bible parable, where a rich man stacks up wealth for himself without having much to report regarding charitable contributions on his Schedule A, Line 13, God leans down from heaven and basically says: "You fool! Tonight you're going to lose your life. Then what will you do with your big tax refund?"

The main point of this parable, of course, is that a man or woman, regardless of income or wealth, needs to maintain a constant attitude of being "rich toward God." But now let's try to get very, very practical. Are we obligated to give to others? Or to God? And if so, how much? Is there a magic formula, a sacred percentage, which will keep our hearts forever linked with God's, and keep us from the fatal mistake of trusting in self?

You probably remember the big headlines when Ted Turner gave a billion dollars to the United Nations. Or maybe the entrepreneur, Charles Feeney, co-founder of Duty Free Shoppers, Limited, who, back in 1984, gave to a charitable foundation something like $500 million in profits — which has since grown into $3.5 billion. Or the two rich kids, David Suna and John Tu, who sold 80% of their computer memory products company, Kingston Technology Corporation, for $1.5 billion . . . and decided to spread out the money in the form of huge bonuses for every single employee on their payroll. And the world applauds, giving these people a big UP arrow. But what does the Bible teach us about giving?

Number One: our giving, our charity, is designed to keep us in a trust relationship with God. It's to keep us depending on Him, acknowledging Him. In fact, all through Luke 12, Christ instructs His listeners to walk in that relationship, to be worry-free as we trust in God. And anytime you and I are tempted to do what this farmer did — to hoard wealth, to pile up more and more and more, to build barns so big that they block our view of the trees and the sky and heaven itself — we're failing to keep ourselves on the highway of trust.

The second, related principle is also found right here in this same Bible passage, way down in verse 48, in a section describing a master who takes a trip and then returns to see what his servants are doing. Here's what Christ says: "From everyone who has been given much, much will be demanded; and from the one who has been entrusted with much, much more will be asked."

Now, this makes sense, first of all, from a practical point of view. The more you're given, the more it's expected that you'll be able to help others. There are those for whom $353 is a huge amount to give to charity; in some countries people don't even earn that much in a year. But if you're the Vice President of the United States, that number sounds kind of small.

Even here in the New Testament is a wonderful little story where Jesus and His disciples see a poor woman creep toward the offering plate at church and silently slip in two little coins — her last two little coins. All around her, Pharisees and millionaires are hiring press agents and brass bands and riding up in limos to drop in their big, big offerings. And then this woman with the two cents puts in what she can. And Christ gives her the warmest of commendations.

Here's the point, though. Not too long after this, in fact, right after the crucifixion and resurrection, rich men like Nicodemus and Joseph of Arimathea joined the new Christian church. And they contributed much larger amounts. It would have been a travesty if they had just put in two cents out of their great abundance. More was expected from them, much more, and they came through with flying colors.

Whatever our station in life is, we need to give enough to accomplish two things. First of all, to be doing our fair share. And secondly, enough so that we'll continue in a relationship of dependence on God's mercy and not on our money.

I've always appreciated the understated influence of the scholar and writer C. S. Lewis, who was an incredibly successful author back in the 30s, 40s, and 50s. He received a comfortable salary from his job as a Cambridge professor, and then got all those royalties from bestsellers like *Screwtape Letters* and his very popular children's series, *Chronicles of Narnia*. And yet he lived quite simply there at The Kilns with his brother Warnie. Where was all of the money going? Well, a great deal of it went to charities which he quietly supported. And sometimes if a friend or even a letter-writing correspondent he had never met was in need of help, Lewis would quietly notify his publisher that so-and-so was to receive a monthly stipend out of his royalties. No fanfare, no headlines. Just a quiet Christian doing what was not only the right thing, but also a valuable way to keep himself humble and teachable and trusting in his own God.

Interestingly he didn't write much about money himself or about how much a person ought to contribute. But in his classic book, *Mere Christianity,* which had to have brought him another flood of income, he makes this comment: "Charity — giving to the poor — is an essential part of Christian morality: in the frightening parable of the sheep and the goats it seems to be the point on which everything turns. . . . I do not believe one can settle how much we ought to give. I am afraid the only safe rule is to give more than we can spare. In other words, if our expenditure on comforts, luxuries, amusements, etc., is up to the standard common among those with the same income as our own, we are probably giving away too little. If our charities do not at all pinch or hamper us, I should say they are too small. There ought to be things we should like to do and cannot do because our charitable expenditure excludes them. . . . For many of us the great obstacle to charity lies not in our luxurious living or desire for more money, but in our fear — fear of insecurity."

Maybe we should all think about this. Does our giving ever pinch? Do we ever contribute so much that we have to do without something we'd really like — in fact, something that we honestly deserve after all the hard work we've done?

But did you also notice how he addressed the issue of trust and insecurity? That's why we hoard money! That's why we build up such big nest eggs we could never spend them. We don't know how much rain is coming, which is why we pile up lots and lots and lots more for that proverbial rainy day. And so the Word of God teaches us to give, to share, to let go, to simply fall into the hands of God.

I guess this subject wouldn't be complete if we didn't visit the Bible passage you've probably been expecting us to tour all along. Yes, it's found in the last book of the Old Testament: Malachi 3. And just as the parable of the Sheep and the Goats — which C. S. Lewis just referred to — has God taking a very hard and penetrating look at how generous His professed followers are, these words are even more straightforward.

"Will a man rob God? Yet you rob Me. But you ask, 'How do we rob You?' In tithes and offerings. You are under a curse — the whole nation of you — because you are robbing Me. Bring the whole tithe into the storehouse, that there may be food in My house."

Many Christians today believe and practice the Bible custom of tithing, where they give a full ten percent of their income to the work of God. Now, that's a matter between you and the Lord. But I'd like to suggest that the Bible concept of tithing does two things very effectively. First of all, it is a wonderful way to make sure that everyone pays their fair share. A Wall Street millionaire pays much more than a kid making minimum wage. In fact, many of them can and do give far more than 10%. Secondly, tithing — paying the Lord a substantial amount like 10% — is generally enough to help us keep trusting God. For too many of us, a dollar a week tossed into the plate on Sabbath or Sunday morning simply doesn't accomplish that. But tithing, calculating out of your income, your increase, and then giving to the Lord that ten percent, is a good way to keep God first and to practice a mindset of full dependence.

In fact, God says so Himself! "'Test Me in this,' says the Lord Almighty, 'and see if I will not throw open the floodgates of heaven and pour out so much blessing that you will not have room enough for it."

Isn't it ironic? This rich farmer had full barns — by being selfish. And then lost everything. But here God promises us fuller barns, overflowing barns, bursting over barns . . . if we'll deliberately practice unselfishness and giving.

I say again: it's upside-down math! You've got to love it.

Sorority Girls Who Missed the Wedding

31. Flight Delays on Virgin Atlantic

32. An Extra Can of O's

33. A Quaker State of Mind

34. Doing Pushups Ahead of Time

35. Always Ready For a Fire Drill

FLIGHT DELAYS ON VIRGIN ATLANTIC

It was the high-flying corporate opportunity of a lifetime, and J.B. (short for Jackson Bishop Silvestri) had swung into gear in a nanosecond. Parable Enterprises had a shot at landing two contracts totaling $118 million with the British government, but the twin proposals had to be at Number Ten Downing Street by ten a.m. the next morning. Delivered in person, of course. And this was a case of starting from scratch.

Well, there was no time to lose. From his Paris suite at the Hotel George V, J.B. picked up his phone, and with one terse phone call, put the emergency plan into effect. Team A, five top company reps, was already at the home office in New York, and Team B, based in Dallas, would link up with them there. The Terrific Ten, he always called them, would fly out that same evening, Kennedy to Heathrow nonstop — on Virgin Atlantic, of course — drafting the twin proposals as they went. Flight #4 would land at 7:10 a.m., giving them time to freshen up, grab a jolt of caffeine, zip out the 100 or so pages on a laser printer for rent at Heathrow's business center, and catch a company limo over to Prime Minister Tony Blair's offices. Nothing to it . . . and ten sky-high, last-minute plane tickets wagered against a possible payoff of $118 million was a bet old J.B. would take any day of the week.

Well, the Terrific Ten — and these ladies were the best in the business — got on board, fastened their seatbelts, put their tray tables and seat backs in the full and upright locked position, and waited impatiently for Virgin Atlantic to get ten minutes into its flight so that they could boot up their Pentium-powered, high-speed laptop computers. And as soon as the pilot gave them the go-ahead, the fingers began to fly. Ninety words a minute, proposals and flow charts and Microsoft PowerPoint visuals with little logos flying through the screen with screeching brake noises. They barely touched their dinners, they didn't watch the movie, and they didn't

look out the windows, except for Windows 98 and the $118 mil-
lion report taking shape on the ten screens.

Just as the plane began to dip down from its assigned flying alti-
tude of 33,000 feet, and with the morning sun barely breaking over
the horizon of the Atlantic Ocean and the distant profile of the
coast of Ireland, the batteries on the ten laptop computers began to
beep. The juice was just about gone. Well, this was expected; the
Terrific Ten knew full well how long a battery pack would last.
And they also had known that once they got to Heathrow, they had
about an hour and a half where they could plug in and finish up the
report before jumping in the limo.

And then all at once they heard those dreaded words come crack-
ling through the plane's speakers and through all the headsets as
people were watching a Sky Report from NBC News. "Ladies and
gentlemen, we're experiencing some delay with Heathrow. There's
quite a stack of planes below us with the morning traffic, and
Tower Control is asking us to circle. It may be about 45 minutes,
perhaps even a bit longer. We'll keep you posted."

What?! One of the ladies from Parable Enterprises — on the B
team — looked down at her watch. Forty-five minutes? That was
pretty much all of their cushion. They needed that time on the
ground where there was juice flowing at 220 volts. How were they
going to finish their reports and get them to the Prime Minister?
"Are you almost done with your section?" another one of them
asked her seatmate. "No," she said, shaking her head. "I've got to
have at least another 30, 40 minutes to summarize."

"How much time left on your laptop?"

"It's out. I just saved everything and shut down so I wouldn't lose
my files."

"I'm out too." And the young lady, Deirdre, undid her seatbelt so she could see across to the other side of the big widebody jet where the other team was still working away, clicking along at 90 words a minute. "Hey! Aren't your batteries running out?"

Carol, the team leader for the New York group, gave a little shrug. "Yeah, they did. But we packed along spare batteries just in case we hit a delay up here. So it's no big deal."

"You did what?"

Carol hit the "save" button on her document. "We brought along extra battery packs. We ordered them from CompUSA, and they pop right in. That way we can go eight hours instead of four. Don't you have them too?"

Deirdre felt her face going flush. "Uh . . . well, no. I guess we never thought of it." And then she kind of gulped. "Any chance you have a second spare? Otherwise, there's no way we'll finish our half." Right at that moment the captain came on again to let them know that a landing slot might open up, but for sure it was going to make them at least an hour late . . . and that traffic going into London was bumper-to-bumper. A big groan went up from the packed Virgin Atlantic plane.

Once they were on the ground, Parable Enterprises' special task force, the Terrific Ten, found itself now in two groups: the five with foresight, and the five foolish Virgin Atlantic passengers who were still looking for a wall outlet. And while they looked, the A Team, five women who had their reports complete, rendezvoused with the boss, J.B., got into a long black limousine, sank into the genuine leather seats, and said to the driver: "Take us to Tony's place, please."

"Jolly good," said the chauffeur as he pulled onto the expressway.

*   *   *

I guess maybe that's how Jesus would have told that story today. In Matthew 25, it has a more dusty flavor to it, with primitive lamps that go out and a wedding feast in a Judean village. But there's still a scene where someone runs out of an important resource — in the Bible it's oil for the lamp — and where someone misses the ride of their lifetime.

Matthew's version is right in the middle of a long, long section of Scripture running three full chapters, where Jesus is teaching people about His own Second Coming and the importance of being ready. Here's the story, and it starts the same way most of His parables do:

"At that time the kingdom of heaven will be like . . . ten virgins who took their lamps and went out to meet the bridegroom. Five of them were foolish and five were wise. The foolish ones took their lamps but did not take any oil with them. The wise, however, took oil in jars along with their lamps. The bridegroom was a long time in coming, and they all became drowsy and fell asleep."

Now, let's hit the pause button already and ask: do you see the parallels? Aside from the word "virgins" and my very subtle choice of airlines earlier? Ten young ladies are heading to a very important event, and there's a delay. They end up waiting longer than they thought. And the group ends up being split demographically right down the middle: Wise and Foolish. What made the difference? One group planned ahead and had juice, the other didn't. It was a case of being prepared; it's as simple as that.

This much is clear already: being ready for the coming of Jesus isn't an automatic thing. People may debate what kind of preparation is necessary, but Jesus teaches that *some* kind certainly is. You can be ready, or you can be not ready. And in many of these mysterious, flavor-filled, hidden-meaning stories we call the parables of Jesus, a common theme shows itself: *people who miss out.* Not everyone gets into the wedding feast; some are left out. No

wonder our kids sing at Christian summer camp: "Give me oil in my lamp; KEEP me burning. Give me oil in my lamp, I pray."
I guess readiness, then, is our theme and our prayer in discussing this topic: *Sorority Girls Who Missed the Wedding*. Or in this case, computer whizzes who missed the limo!

Back when this message first aired on the radio, it was a June 22, 1998. And I couldn't help but notice that on that very date in history, June 22, way back in the year 1807, something happened that had quite a major impact on a still virgin country called the United States of America. A U.S. frigate sailing about 40 miles out of Chesapeake Bay — in fact, the ship was called the *Chesapeake* — was fired upon by the crew of a British man-of-war vessel, the *Leopard*. Troops from the enemy vessel boarded the *Chesapeake*, and won the day partly because the commander of the American ship, a Captain James Barron, was unprepared for battle. He simply wasn't ready, and the English troops came aboard.

That June 22 event, just a footnote in history today, is one of the factors that eventually led to the War of 1812. The *Chesapeake*'s commander, James Barron, later faced a court-martial and was actually convicted for the crime of being unprepared. In parable terms, his lamp had gone out; his laptop computer was dead. And two nations went to war.

No wonder Jesus closes with this warning, which makes good sense whether you're flying Virgin Atlantic, or down here below waiting for the Second Coming: "Therefore keep watch, because you do not know the day or the hour."

32
AN EXTRA CAN OF O'S

They say that when you're huddled in a tent at Camp Four on Everest, you really don't need much by way of food. Most would-be summiteers on the world's highest mountain, when they get up there in the Death Zone, at 26,000 feet, and are about ready to head out for that killer 18-hour climb to the peak and back, simply can't force down any more food. The human body is so thrashed, it just can't take in nourishment. You eat when you get back down — if you get back down.

So when you plan for an assault on Everest, you can go light on the menu. But there's one other area where expedition climbers always, always, *always* make sure they have plenty of supplies.

In his book, *The Climb*, Russian climber Anatoli Boukreev describes the endless wrangling to line up a huge shipment, $30,000 worth, of this precious commodity. And of course, I'm talking about oxygen. He had a connection in Moscow who manu-factured the very latest. These bottles, made by a company called Poisk, were almost a full pound lighter in weight than anything the competition could come up with. So after a lot of politics and threatening and price-undercutting, the Mountain Madness expedi-tion headed by Scott Fischer bought a total of 55 Poisk three-liter bottles, 54 Zvesda four-liter bottles, 14 regulators, and 14 masks. The state-of-the-art Poisk bottles, the ones the climbers would use near the top, cost an incredible $325 each. Planning for three bot-tles per climber just on Summit Day . . . well, you can do the math for yourself.

One thing was for sure: you didn't want to run out of oxygen — or O's, as the top climbers called the bottled air. We've shared on radio broadcasts several tragedy-laden stories from books like Jon Krakauer's bestseller, *Into Thin Air*, and some of the spiritual les-sons to be found at 29,028 feet. And this is one lesson many climbers have learned the hard way. In fact, we should really say "the late Scott Fischer," and now also "the late Anatoli Boukreev." Both men are dead, their bodies frozen high on the Himalayas.

In Matthew 25, the story Jesus tells happens in warmer climates, and there's more oxygen in the Galilean air, but the stakes are just as high. Five girls plan ahead, and have the precious ingredient of oil. They have plenty and to spare. Five foolish ones don't.

But it might be well, first of all, to notice what the ten virgins all had in common. First, all ten girls are waiting with the same goal in mind. They all want to see the Bridegroom. In spiritual terms, they all want to meet God. They all are seeking Him, looking for Jesus' soon return. At least as far as that goes, they are all wise, all ten of them. Jesus told some stories where people couldn't even be bothered to show up for the wedding, but not here. All ten of these women have good motives.

All ten had lamps. And as so many of us like to figure out what everything represents, right down to the flavor of the wedding cake, it's suggested that these lamps represent the Word of God. Actually, Psalm 119:105 uses that very metaphor: "Thy Word is a lamp unto my feet, and a light unto my path."

Is it possible, then, that a man or woman might actually be looking for Jesus to come, and also have a Bible on the coffee table . . . and still somehow be lost? Jesus certainly tells the story with that warning in mind. But first, let's see what else all ten virgins have in common.

Notice: all ten of them go to sleep. Verse 5: "The bridegroom was a long time in coming, and they all became drowsy and fell asleep."

The foolish five went to sleep, and finally, so did the wise ones too. And that's a hard point to apply. Is it all right for Christians,

God's people who eagerly await His coming, to get discouraged and spiritually go to sleep? Well, no, I certainly don't want to say that. And the Bible shares a great abundance of verses that talk about not sleeping, about not dozing, about staying awake and alert. In our last parable, we were in Luke 12, and in a Bible section called "Watchfulness," Jesus has this warning: "Be dressed ready for service and keep your lamps burning, like men waiting for their master to return from a wedding banquet, so that when he comes and knocks they can immediately open the door for him. It will be good for those servants whose master finds them watching when he comes."

And certainly we all remember that sad, real story — not a parable — in the Garden of Gethsemane, where Jesus begged and pleaded for just one disciple to stay awake with Him. But not one of His friends seemed to be able to do so.

And yet here in this story, even the good girls are asleep. There's a delay; it gets to be midnight, even, and they just can't stay awake.

Let me ask this: has there been a delay in Jesus' coming? If your grandparents were Christians, did they expect our Lord's return many years ago? Of course they did. My own grandfather, evangelist Dan Venden, never thought he'd be in his retirement years, and he's been resting in a grave now for more than 25 years. Some of you may remember how in the early 60s, a young Billy Graham told reporters: "I don't want to set dates, but I don't see how Christ's coming can be delayed more than five years off in the future."

The disciples pretty much felt the same way. Five years, maybe ten. But there's been a long delay, and here we are. We figure it's almost midnight for sure now, spiritually speaking, but no one knows, do they? That's one of the biggest lessons of this parable, and one Jesus explicitly states in verse 13. "You do not know the day or the hour." How many times have people missed those nine plain words?

And as we weigh all of the stories of Jesus, and sort out the details and the interpretations, it's clear that there's a kind of sleeping that is all right and a kind that's not. "Be alert!" Jesus says. "Stay awake!" But here in Matthew 25, even the wise virgins did fall asleep when there was a delay.

I'd like to share a helpful note from the *Tyndale New Testament Commentaries* for Matthew, which are edited by Dr. Richard T. France of London Bible College. See what you think: "During the 'delay,'" he writes, and that's certainly where we are right now, "life must go on, and we cannot live on constant alert. The difference was whether they [the ten virgins] had already prepared for the summons, or had left preparation to the last minute, when it would be too late."

Now it would be easy to go off track right here. I don't really want to say that we should not live on "constant alert." But we can't live forever in breathless expectancy. However, it's certainly true that a Christian can and should be prepared, with extra oil or Poisk oxygen tanks, whatever they represent in spiritual terms. And then this parable suggests that it's appropriate for that same Christian to continue life in calm but joyful readiness. When bed-times come, it's all right to sleep. When witnessing opportunities present themselves, we take them. *Life isn't marked by franticness, it's marked by faithfulness.* As long as the oxygen or the oil is right there at the ready.

Maybe you remember the old story, where a great and aged saint of God was hoeing in his garden one day. And then a detractor hooted at him. "What would you do if Christ were to come in five minutes?" And so the story goes, the Christian saint straightened up and said with great calm: "Finish hoeing this row." Because he was ready. He was looking for his Savior's return, and there was no need to panic.

On the other side of the great divide, I remember a friend, a coworker right here at our Adventist Media Center. In his younger years, he struggled mightily with the concept of being ready. He wasn't just awake; his whole body and soul were twitching with fear and anticipation. Was he prepared for Jesus' return? Were there any unforgiven sins in his life?

In fact, he went to a private, right-wing kind of Bible college where people learned to focus constantly on their own characters, their holiness or lack of holiness. How good were they being, how obedient? In all honesty, this young man actually began to do without sleep. He would fast and skip meals, and then determine to stay awake all night in prayer. According to how he interpreted this story in Matthew 25, if he was to be ready to meet the Bridegroom, he had to be awake at all times. "Watch and pray," the Bible had said, and so this meant being up and alert 24 hours a day.

Well, I thank God that the gospel of grace finally came flooding into this sincere man; today he's a powerful gospel preacher for Jesus, presenting a balanced message of watchfulness and joyful rest in Christ. He's prepared, with extra oil at his side and his lamp burning at all times.

So as we look at the similarities between these two groups, we see that they're all looking for the return of the Bridegroom. They all have a kind of religious life, a lamp, which might mean that they're holding onto Bibles, even reading them. When there's a delay, they all relax and sleep, which apparently can be all right too, as long as alarm clocks work correctly.

But when the buzzer does go off, we come upon the one great difference. And what a deadly difference!

33
A QUAKER STATE OF MIND

Maybe you remember an old cowboy picture from a few years ago, where Billy Crystal and a couple of friends are on a wild west vacation, driving a herd of cows from one state to another one. And Curly, the crusty old cowhand who was leading the way (and also scaring the clients to death with his macho-rattlesnake demeanor) entered into a bit of one-syllable philosophizing with Crystal. "Life really boils down to one thing," he said at last, holding up one finger mysteriously. "Just one thing." Well, what was the one thing? Despite his fears, Billy really wanted to know.

And then the answer: "I'm not going to tell you."

"What?!"

"Nope. You have to figure it out for yourself."

And in this parable of Jesus, we kind of come down to the same thing — and it's a bit maddening. In the story of the five wise virgins and the five foolish ones, the point is to teach about the concept of preparedness. The five smart ones have extra oil for their lamps, and the foolish ones don't. The five with oil go to the wedding feast, and the others are lost. So immediately we ask the obvious and important question: what does the oil represent? Because those who have it are saved, and those who don't have it are lost. And yet, in all 13 verses devoted to this anecdote, Jesus never mentions or even hints about what the all-important ingredient stands for. It's like a joke with the punch line missing.

The wise and patient Bible student can't help but notice that when a man or woman asks this question, "What must I do to be saved?", several different answers are given. Paul and Silas, talking to a jailor in Philippi, said very simply, "Just believe on the Lord Jesus Christ." A man asking Jesus got this answer instead:

"Keep all the commandments — and also sell all your belongings in order to be able to follow Me." Another man who asked the same question of the same Teacher, Jesus, got a third, completely different answer: "Love God with all your heart, and your neighbor as yourself. Be a good neighbor." In another parable of Christ's, a man had to have on a certain wedding garment in order to attain salvation. And here in Matthew 25, hidden in the subliminal threads of this story, is a fifth message: "You have to have an extra supply of lamp oil — whatever lamp oil is — in order to get into the wedding feast."

So how do we sort this out and solve the riddle of the oil? It might be helpful to work backwards, as detectives sometimes do, and study by the process of elimination. What is this story *not* telling us?

Again, here were ten virgins who did many things the same. What does it take to be saved? Well, all ten of these girls professed a membership in the wedding party, so to speak. All ten were planning to be there. All ten were out in the city square or in the street where the bridegroom was to be coming. Could we say, then, that mere profession or church membership isn't enough? "Oh, I've been a Christian all my life," someone says. That statement, all by itself, doesn't indicate that a person is going to be saved.

There's been a suggestion that the lamps these women had with them are significant, that they could represent the Word of God. And maybe that's true. Does having a Bible in your house or even in your hand prove that you're a saved person? Obviously not; some of the greatest enemies of the Christian faith memorize huge portions of Scripture for the purpose of debate and destruction.

As it got late in the evening in this story, all ten women fell asleep. When it was midnight and the siren sounded, all ten woke up. And the five foolish virgins, even at that crucial moment, were still very interested in going to the wedding. We could interpret this to mean that there will be people at the very end who look up in the clouds, see the King of kings returning, and honestly think they are going to be saved. They want to be saved; they scurry around to do whatever it takes at that moment. So their desires are good . . . and yet, for some reason, they are not saved. When the door to the banquet hall is shut, they're on the outside.

Well, we still haven't uncovered the truth, but we can prayerfully surmise here that church membership is not the answer. Carrying Bibles and even reading Bibles may not be the whole answer. Thinking you're saved doesn't always prove that you are. This is very unsettling, maybe, and so we come back to that oil. Clearly the oil has something to do with preparedness, with having something in reserve. But what? And of course, the stakes are as high as stakes can be, aren't they? This is a life-and-death Bible study!

Fortunately, our Bibles do provide us with two wonderful clues, and one of them is right here in the story. But let's take the other one first. In the Old Testament book of Zechariah, this prophet of Israel has a dream. In fact, the whole book is basically a dream, but this part is in chapter four. "[The angel] asked me, 'What do you see?' I answered, 'I see a solid gold lampstand with a bowl at the top and seven lights on it, with seven channels to the lights. . . . Also there are two olive trees by it, one on the right of the bowl and the other on its left.'"

Just a bit later in this beautiful chapter, the Bible describes a flow of golden oil from those two olive trees. Then in verse 6 Zechariah asks the angel: "What are these things?"

"Don't you know?" the angel responds. And then this magnificent verse: "Not by might nor by power, but by My Spirit,' says the Lord Almighty."

And Bible scholars affirm that the oil in this great vision represents the power of the Holy Spirit.

Now as we move back across time to the New Testament, and this story of warning by Jesus, what does it mean if we give the parable this application? Could the oil for these lamps similarly represent the Holy Spirit?

Consider again that here are ten women: all in the church. All watching for the coming of the Bridegroom. All of them signed up for the wedding. All of them toting Bibles. But only five of the ten have a spiritual relationship that's alive — because they have the Holy Spirit. Only five are living in daily connection with the Bridegroom. Only five are reading those Bibles in such a way that they are really becoming acquainted with its subject.

Let me go a step further. I'd suggest to you that only five of these ten are really — as we say nowadays — "walking the walk," instead of just "talking the talk." Their connection to Christ, because of the Holy Spirit, the oil, is a faith in action. They not only claim the name of Christ, but they try to live as He lived. They follow His example in obedience and in doing good in the world around them; in fact, the rest of this chapter proves that very point with two more famous parables.

In a classic old book from about a hundred years ago, entitled *Christ's Object Lessons*, Ellen White talks about the oil for these lamps.

"Into the hearts of all who are united to God by faith, the golden oil of love flows freely, to shine out again in good works, in real, heartfelt service for God."

Do you know what she's writing about? This very story: the parable of the ten virgins. And it's interesting that those who have the oil, the presence of the Holy Spirit, have an active faith, "shining out in good works, in service." These five wise watchers and seekers don't just say the name of Jesus and carry around His dusty book. They know Him intimately! The Holy Spirit has invigorated their religious experience; their faith is a real relationship where they are trusting a Savior they actually know.

In fact, let me be rather bold. The best thing we could say is that this oil, this reserve, IS knowing Jesus. Period. True, the Bible may describe it as the presence of the Holy Spirit. But why did Jesus send the Holy Spirit after He went back to heaven? To keep us connected with Him! "I'll send the Holy Spirit in My place," He promised. The Holy Spirit illuminates our minds as we read Scripture looking for Jesus! The Holy Spirit fills us with the thoughts and the attitudes of Christ, giving us, as Paul describes it, "the mind of Christ"!

And I did mention a second clue regarding the oil in this parable. Is it indeed the Holy Spirit which makes our faith real and living, which gives us an intimate friendship with Christ instead of a dry, formal, theoretical shell of impersonal religion? Let's cut right to the finish line, where Christ wraps up the parable. Matthew 25:11: "The virgins who were ready [with their oil] went in with [the bridegroom] to the wedding banquet. And the door was shut. Later the others also came. 'Sir! Sir!' they said. 'Open the door for us!' But he replied, 'I tell you the truth, I DON'T KNOW YOU.' Therefore keep watch, because you do not know the day or the hour" (emphasis supplied).

So what is the oil? It is to know Jesus! In this story, the ones who had it knew Jesus and He knew them. That's the bottom line right there. The oil was the ingredient of relationship, of friend-ship, of trust, of biblical faith that is a constant "leaning on the everlasting arms" and not just a Greek word in a concordance.

So how much do we need the oil then? In this Bible story, it was everything! Knowing the Bridegroom was everything! And it's the same today. Like those climbers on Everest who absolutely must have oxygen and don't take one step toward the summit with-out it, we must have the oil: a Spirit-led, Spirit-strengthened friendship with Jesus.

34

DOING PUSHUPS AHEAD OF TIME

I'm going to wear you out right here, make you feel tired, with an old football story from the archives. *Instant Replay* was written as a diary by Green Bay Packer Jerry Kramer to chronicle the 1967 season. And of course, back in those glory days, there was a certain short, red-faced, screaming Italian coach in charge named Mr. Vincent Lombardi.

The book really starts with the pre-season practice session, which runs eight weeks. The Packers held their camps at St. Norbert College in West De Pere, Wisconsin, ten minutes away from Green Bay. Two players to a tiny dorm room — these big, hulking 270-pounders sleeping on short little beds built for college freshman English majors.

But then there were the practice sessions themselves. And by the admission of everyone in the league, nobody practiced like the Packers. The team went through "two-a-days," double workout sessions to get in shape. As Kramer describes it, "the agony was beyond belief." There was a drill called "up-downs," where the whole team would be running in place, lifting their knees as high in the air as they could for 20, 30, sometimes 40 seconds. Then the coach would shout: "Down!" And the whole team would flop down on the grass, their stomachs smacking the ground. "Up!" And they'd run in place. "Down!" "Up!" And sometimes they'd do that 60 or 70 times until everyone on the team was gasping in exhaustion.

Of course, this is mid-July in Wisconsin, if you can imagine the heat and humidity. And this just went on and on and on. Kramer tells how a big kid named Leon Crenshaw, a rookie, showed up at camp weighing 315 pounds. One day in the cafeteria, after doing about 80 of those "up-downs," Crenshaw just flat-out fainted. Passed out cold on the floor. He'd lost 25 pounds in two weeks.

Another kid came to Kramer, his tongue hanging out down to his toes. "How do you do it?" he asked. "I can't hack it."

"You've got to block out the pain," the veteran told him. "Just don't think about it. Don't stop for anything."

"Yeah," the rookie said, "but man, I see visions out there."

"What do you mean?"

And the kid repeated: "Visions, man. I see people walking around in the air." He was literally hallucinating. And Kramer adds a little P.S. "He got cut from the team a few days later."

Here's a bit more pain, though. Jerry Kramer, being a right guard, was a huge guy, weighing in at around 260. But he usually liked to play more at about 245, so it was a season-long struggle to get down to that weight. (That's a thought, isn't it — getting *down* to 245?) So he'd sit in the cafeteria with the other players, some of the tight ends eating huge steaks with gravy and butter and rolls and ice cream. And Kramer would eat the tiniest little piece of meat, and a small dish of peas and one glass of iced tea, and eat it all as slowly as he could, to make it seem like more food.

Well, here's the point. All of this exercise — the "up-downs," the grass sprints, the dieting — was for one purpose. Playing a better game! That added tenth-of-a-second of speed off the line when the center snapped the ball. That little advantage of power, of raw linebacker strength for when he had to face his old archrival, Alex Karras of the Detroit Lions, or Jethro Pugh of the hated Dallas Cowboys. But who could know if all that training and dieting would ever pay off big? Green Bay might win or lose every game by three touchdowns. Would it ever happen that all the agony, the preparing, the sweating and the crying and the pushing and enduring Lombardi's screaming fits would ever culminate in one big play that made all the difference?

Well, some of you football fans will know the answer. To this day they call it the Ice Bowl, where on December 31, they had to face the Cowboys for the NFC championship. Thirteen degrees below zero there in Green Bay. And the game came down to the very last minute, with the Packers behind, 17-14, driving for a TD. They got down to the enemy one-yard line, botched two plays, finally slid down to the *one-foot* line and had one last shot. No time-outs left. They could have tried for a field goal to tie, but decided to go for the win right there. A quarterback sneak, a 31-wedge, with Bart Starr carrying the ball. And it was going to be Jerry Kramer who had to open up the hole. He simply had to get Jethro Pugh out of the way.

And Kramer writes how he poured everything he had into that one block. All the up-downs, the exercising, the relentless grinding of practice, practice, practice . . . and all the dieting to keep in perfect shape . . . all the endless drills of blocking, pushing, moving your man out . . . it all went into that last block. He blocked Pugh outside and Bart Starr churned into the opening and fell across the finish line. The Green Bay Packers were the champs again, and on TV sets all around the world, on instant replay — that's the title of his book — people saw that block by #64, Jerry Kramer, over and over and over again.

Well, there's football, which is a game . . . and then there's this thing called Christianity and the challenge of living in these last days. And Jesus tells a story which seems to hint at "up-downs" and glasses of iced tea. Because here in Matthew 25 there are five wise virgins who are prepared for the big game, and there are five foolish girls who aren't. Five have trained and five haven't. Here's verse 6 and following:

"At midnight the cry rang out: 'Here's the bridegroom! Come out to meet him!' Then all the virgins woke up and trimmed their lamps. The foolish ones said to the wise, 'Give us some of your oil; our lamps are going out.' 'No,' they replied, 'there may not be enough for both us and you. Instead, go to those who sell oil and buy some for yourselves.' But while they were on their way to buy the oil, the bridegroom arrived. The virgins who were ready went in with him to the wedding banquet. And the door was shut."

Notice how the five girls ask the others for help. "Give us some of your oil." And it's not that the wise ones are selfish; it's just an impossible thing they're being asked to do. They barely have enough for themselves.

Let's ask this: can one person prepare spiritually for another? Can someone else stock your oil? Or do all your pushups in training for the Super Bowl? That's not possible, is it? Every Christian has to have their own walk with Jesus. Every believer has to nurture his or her own relationship with God. I noticed in the Seventh-day Adventist Bible commentary for this story a good line: "Character is not transferable. One Christian cannot do for another that which he must do for himself in preparation for the crisis that lies ahead."

And consider this too. There's a time to get ready and do your exercises and stock up your oil. And that time is *before* the crisis, before the midnight hour. A good Green Bay Packer couldn't come up to December 31, five or six hours before the kickoff of that championship game with Dallas, and think to himself: "Oh my, I'd better do a few pushups here, and jog a lap or two." It's far, far too late by then.

In this story, there was a time to get oil, and that time had past. It's suggested that maybe the five foolish virgins could go buy oil. But at midnight? How many stores were open then? The last I checked, there weren't any 24-hour convenience marts or 7-Elevens in existence in the time of Christ. The end of the story does have these five girls showing up late at the banquet hall, and it doesn't specify if they managed to scrounge some oil somewhere. But when midnight comes, when it's time for the Super Bowl, the hour for preparing has long past. It's now time for the *results* of preparation to manifest themselves.

Do you remember the line by Thomas Fuller? "In fair weather prepare for foul."

Or the ancient philosopher Syrus: "We should lay up in peace what we shall need in war."

What does this mean for us? Training camp is happening now for you and for me. We need to get that oil, the Holy Spirit, flowing right now, today. We need to know Christ today, have a living relationship with Him at this very moment.

I have a missionary friend, Dr. Ralph Neall, who, while we were in Thailand, served for years in Saigon, right during the Vietnam War. So he knows a few things about preparing for crisis ahead of time. In his recent book, entitled *How Long, O Lord?*, he comments: "The reward for the wise is a place at the wedding banquet of the Lamb. The loss of the foolish is to be shut out with the tragic words, 'I don't know you.' If we want Him to know us then, we must know Him now!"

And then he adds: "The parable of the virgins tells us we should cultivate our devotional lives and keep our vessels full of oil every day. We never know when we may find ourselves thrown into a situation in which we won't have time to study and pray before making a decision or giving an answer."

You know, our electronic pocket calendars don't tell us exactly when the Big Game is. "No man knows the day or the hour"; that's the punch line of this story. But we know who the Coach is, and when practice is too. Friend, it's right now. Grab your shoulder pads and let's get out there.

35

ALWAYS READY FOR A FIRE DRILL

An amusing incident took place recently with a number of our Voice of Prophecy staff. We were at a Hyatt Regency hotel in Bellevue, Washington, enjoying a marvelous, funny, rollicking-good-time story being told by my friend Terry Johnson, a former member of President Reagan's Honor Guard. And all at once, while he was entertaining us, a fire alarm went off and a female voice announced through the entire hotel P.A. system, all 25 stories, that the hotel should be evacuated. "Please move to the exits." Well, we started . . . but after just about a minute, someone waved the white flag and said it was a false alarm.

Terry, of course, rolled with the punches, and made a good joke or two about it. But that false alarm set me to thinking again about this story of the big wedding that's delayed until midnight. And there are a lot of false alarms. You know: "Hey, Jesus is coming! I've figured it out with my prophecy charts, and He's going to arrive for sure in the year 1994!" I'm sure you've heard those and so have I. But this very story tells us in clear English that no man, no woman, knows the day or the hour.

So here's our final question: what if it isn't a false alarm? What if the hotel really had been on fire? And suppose Terry Johnson had just kept on talking and preaching? What if all of us sitting around the banquet tables with our half-eaten desserts had just stayed there, not budging out of our seats? What if the waiters had just kept on clearing out the silverware, taking out the food?

The point is this: there's a time for sermons and for dessert and for waiters to do their jobs. Those are all good things. But there's also a time to head for the exits because a hotel is on fire. And what would normally be an activity that indicates wisdom . . . is suddenly foolishness because a time of crisis has come.

The clearest demographic demarcation in the story of the ten virgins is this: Wise and Foolish. Five of these women were wise, and five foolish.

In the chapter right before this one, Matthew 24, is another story about wise and foolish. Here's the heart of it: "Who then is the faithful and WISE servant, whom the master has put in charge of the servants in his household to give them their food at the proper time? It will be good for that servant whose master finds him doing so when he returns."

You know, I learn two lessons from this cryptic story. What makes a person wise in these last days? Well, we're plainly told. *Wisdom is to be doing what we're supposed to be doing at the appointed hour.* This man was in charge of the house, in charge of feeding the staff. When the master comes back, that's what he's doing! And that's wisdom.

If you read down a bit further in this story, Jesus then paints a contrast between this servant and another one who decides that the master's been gone a long time. So he begins to beat up on other people and abuse them. He puts the master out of his mind, assuming that he's gone forever. So here's wisdom, parts one AND two. Wisdom is to be doing what you're supposed to be doing, and it's also to be remembering always your relationship with the master.

Back in Old Testament times the children of Israel had a crisis of faith when Moses went up onto Mount Sinai and didn't come back for about 40 days. And the Israelites gave up on both Moses and God. "Out of sight, out of mind." So they said to Aaron: "Build us a new god, one we can see. We think this God is gone." That was foolishness, wasn't it?

If you've been to Sunday School or Sabbath School very many times, you probably recall another story (and song) where you had "wise" on one side and "foolish" on the other side of the beach volleyball court. A wise man, Jesus said, built his house upon the rock. The foolish man built his on the sand. And when the storm came, guess which house was washed away?

Again let's point out that wisdom is to be doing the right thing. In this case, the right thing is to be building houses on rocks. That was wise. Now, there's nothing especially wicked about building a house on sand, except that when El Ninõs are coming, that's the wrong thing to be doing. That's foolish. And let's also notice what these two builders represent. Jesus says very clearly — we can't miss it:

"Everyone who hears these words of Mine and puts them into practice is like a wise man who built his house on the rock."

So what is wisdom in these last days? To be hearing Jesus' words AND doing them. That's preparedness; that's wisdom. Dr. Richard France, author of the *Tyndale New Testament Commentary* for Matthew, defines wise people in commenting on these two stories: "Those who are engaged in action appropriate to their professed status."

He adds another insight which applies to both of these stories: "It is the crisis which will divide the ready from the unready."

Isn't that painfully true? I guess it would actually be all right to build a house on the sand; after all, the view of the beach from there would be terrific. And it's no problem to build there . . . as long as a storm never comes. It would be all right to never really train hard for football, as long as every game you were in was never close or crucial. It would be all right to not have extra oxygen on Everest as long as no storms came along and you didn't climb very high. You could do without extra oil while waiting for the Bridegroom, as long as He wasn't late. But if a crisis comes — and of course, the Bible tells us flat out that there will be one at the midnight hour — there are going to be wise people who have prepared, and foolish ones who haven't.

As we get down to these last moments in our seventh and final parable, let me get just as practical as I can. We talk about oil and oxygen and pushups, and maybe you begin wondering: "But what do I really DO? I want to be wise, but what do I DO each Sunday, Monday, Tuesday, Wednesday, Thursday, Friday, and Saturday?"

In *How Long, O Lord?*, Dr. Ralph Neall discusses how the second coming of Jesus has certainly been delayed. So how can we be ready? And you know, he takes us right to this very chapter we've been studying. According to him, the answer is right here, and it's here three times.

There are three parables here: the ten virgins, the three servants who all received different talents, and then the story of the sheep and goats. You remember that one too, I imagine — where some people had fed strangers, given cups of cold water, visited prisoners, clothed the naked . . . and others hadn't. And the Lord divides them up like sheep and goats: those who did and those who didn't. Anyway, here are the three stories.

And these three parables tell us exactly what we should be doing here as midnight approaches. In the story of the ten virgins, the message is clear: we need to know the Bridegroom and have the extra oil of the Holy Spirit empowering our lives. Day by day, wide awake or drowsy, we need to spend time knowing Jesus Christ.

Story number two: the talents. And here we need to be using our gifts for God. If we have five gifts, use them. If we have one, use the one. But again, we keep in mind that the master of the house — our Friend and Savior Jesus — is coming back, and we want to be able to give Him a good report.

Story number three: those sheep and goats. And here the wise person is simply doing in the world what good he or she can do. Be kind to strangers. Care for the widows and orphans. Love your neighbor. Visit someone in prison.

I'm especially impressed by the "calm" of this book. No fear, no pulse-pounding crisis, no panic, no screaming Armageddon headlines. He does make it clear, as Jesus does, that last-minute preparing is impossible. There does come a time when you can't buy oil and when the door to the banquet is closed and locked. But Dr. Neall just quietly writes that if we're doing these three things — knowing Jesus, using our talents, being kind and loving to others — then whether Christ returns in 50 years or tomorrow night at midnight, we'll be ready.

Let's close with a line from the very famous Tom Bodett. Do you remember? "We'll leave the light on for you." How appropriate as we've talked about lamps and oil! And what does that Motel 6 ad slogan imply? "We'll leave the light on for you"?

Well, two things. First of all, the motel staff will be ready for us. It may be late, and yes, the front-desk person might doze off, but when you ring the bell, they'll be ready. Secondly, they'll have a welcoming spirit. They'll be glad to welcome us as guests.

Don't you really want to say the same to our Friend Jesus right now, "I'll have the light on for You"? "Jesus, I'll be ready. Whenever You come, I want to be doing the wise thing, the right thing, the thing appropriate to the time. And Jesus, with all my heart I say this too: You'll be welcome. Please come and check in soon."

.